The Spirit of Herbs:
A Guide to
the Herbal Tarot

CANDIS CANTIN
MICHAEL TIERRA, O.M.D.

U.S. GAMES SYSTEMS, INC.
Publishers   **Stamford, CT 06902 USA**

The Spirit of Herbs:
A Guide to
the Herbal Tarot

All illustrations by Candis Cantin

Library of Congress Catalog Card Number: 91-67474

ISBN 13: 978-0-88079-525-8

This book is not intended to diagnose or prescribe treatment for disease or injury, nor is it a complete guide to the uSe of herbs. A qualified health worker should be consulted in the event of an injury or disease. Further, one should not harvest or ingest herbs without the knowledge of their usages and properties.

10   9   8   7   6   5

Made in China

U.S. GAMES
SYSTEMS, INC

U.S. GAMES SYSTEMS, INC.
179 Ludlow Street
Stamford, CT 06902 USA
www.usgamesinc.com

To
Lonnie Packard
for his constant love and inner peace;
Lesley Tierra
for her encouragement and support;
and
the Great Mother Earth:
Through her love, forgiveness, and compassion,
may she heal us all.

Contents

The Minor Arcana   73

Herbs and the
Herbal Tarot Deck

Medicinal plants are gentle healers of body, mind, and spirit. The Herbal Tarot deck is a useful introduction to the art of herbalism as well as to the mysticism of the tarot. The symbolism of the deck offers understanding on many levels of the healing messages of the plant beings and shows how they can be teachers and healers of body/mind/spirit.

The tarot is a system of revealing the unconscious and energetic processes of the human psyche. To understand it we must think in a symbolic, dream-imaging way rather than in a rational, linear way. The tarot helps us go beyond the chaos of life and see the greater truths that lie within ourselves. In this day and new age, the tarot is a tool not for fortune telling but for taking responsibility for our own lives and creations. Through its symbols, inner knowing and understanding are revealed and we see how we are children and co-creators of the Divine Life-force.

The Herbal Tarot consists of seventy-eight cards including Major Arcana and Minor Arcana cards. The Major Arcana comprise twenty-two cards ranging from The Fool, key 0, to The World, key XXI. These represent the God-self into and through physical manifestation and are the symbols of the basic life energy that we create. This life force has been recognized by the ancients and is called *chi* by the Chinese and *prana* by Hindus. Many of the herbs on the Major Arcana cards are powerful chi enhancers that help us to implement the energies indicated in the cards. When a Major Arcana card comes up in a reading it suggests a life direction and represents broad and general life patterns.

The Minor Arcana comprise fifty-six cards in four suits: swords, wands, cups, and pentacles. Each suit has fourteen cards: ten cards numbered ace through ten and four court cards—king, queen, knight, and page. The Minor Arcana represent more specific situations and energies. When the Minor Arcana cards come up, they show what actions are needed to work through the current situation.

A layout of cards is like a mandala that can be meditated upon and allowed to permeate your being. Let the colors, forms, and feelings of the cards be your guides as you and those you counsel explore the inner realms.

Plant Meditations

Meditations with plants is a very powerful practice for tapping into ancient and many times dormant knowledge about the plant kingdom's healing ways.

Plant meditations can be done with a card from the Herbal Tarot deck or with trees, herbs, bushes, and houseplants. If you do not have the live plants nearby, you can visualize the plant or look at a picture of it. If you have the plant on hand then place yourself close to the plant so that you are in its auric field. Sometimes you may feel where the plant's aura begins by putting your hands out toward the plant. If you are meditating with a tree, place your back right against its trunk.

Observe the plant for a while and see how it is shaped and take in its color and scent. Then close your eyes and ask the plant if you can enter into its space. When you have its permission, allow your consciousness to be one with the plant. Be silent for a while. If you have a question for the plant, ask it and listen from your heart for the answer. The answer may come as a mental picture, an intuitive or emotional feeling, or a body sensation. Acknowledge and accept this. Ask the plant if it needs anything from you. Acknowledge this and tell the plant that you will do what it has asked of you. End the meditation with a chant, recitation of the mantra *om*, or with whatever makes you comfortable.

Spiritual Properties of Herbs

The information about the spiritual properties of the herbs was gathered from intuition and experimentation, and is not conclusive. We hope that whoever partakes of the herbs for spiritual purposes will follow their own feelings and insights into the plant's energies. The use of plants for spiritual purposes has been lost to Western people for some time but is slowly being rediscovered. We feel confident that it will be a part of routine healing practices in years to come.

Herbal Formulas

Taking an herb or a combination of herbs will create a physical effect as well as a corresponding spiritual effect. This is because the vibration of the plant creates a healing resonance in the body/mind/spirit complex. However, making complicated herbal remedies may be a bit much for the beginner so it is best for the novice to use herbal essences. An herbal essence is made by taking a drop of an herbal extract (called a tincture) and diluting it in one ounce of pure water. Four or more drops of essence are placed under the tongue and allowed to rest for sixty seconds. The vibrational quality of the plant will enter you and will be the seed for the transformation that you wish to undergo. Essences are mild and do not have the medicinal strength larger herbal doses may have but they can act as catalysts for the changes desired. While using an essence, try to have on hand the actual plant or a picture of the plant. This will help you to enter into a rapport with the plant deva, or spirit, and the healing vibrations.

If you wish to put together an herbal medicine formula based on the herbs that turn up in a reading then it may be best to consult an herb book, such as *The Way of Herbs*, by Michael Tierra, or an herbalist to make sure that the amounts and combinations are appropriate.

Poisonous, Toxic, or Psychedelic Plants

Some plants on the Herbal Tarot are poisonous, toxic, or may be classified as psychedelic drugs. DO NOT TAKE ANY OF THE POISONOUS HERBS EXCEPT AS PREPARED BY A REPUTABLE HERBALIST OR HERB COMPANY. Only specific processing renders a poisonous herb nontoxic. The herb aconite, for example, is specially prepared in Chinese formulas, but if taken fresh or dried and made it into a tea or tincture it would cause great pain and death.

Other herbs such as marijuana and poppy are considered psychedelic or narcotic, and in most states are illegal. It is at your discretion as to whether or not to ingest these drugs but meditations with the plants or with a picture of the plants may be quite useful and enlightening.

There are herbs that may be harmful to pregnant women or people with other types of conditions so make sure to consult the medicinal properties of the plants before taking them.

Healing by Herbal Talismans and Charms

Herbal talismans and charms have been used for thousands of years to help people to invoke the powers of protection and to reaffirm and encourage a physical/spiritual healing. To make a talisman, you can take a small pinch of one or more of the herbs that have come up in a given reading and wrap them into a natural fiber pouch which is then worn or carried. This can be part of a ritual or ceremony as complicated or simple as the healer feels comfortable with executing. Traditionally, since herbs possess the power to attract and hold the intention of the healer, herbalists and shamans have communicated their intention by quickly blowing on the talisman before giving it to the receiver. A candle can be lit, a special type of incense or "smudge" can be wafted over the charm, or a chant can be sung as part of the psychic energizing of the charm. These are only some of many possibilities.

The idea is that, first, there is deep communication to the subconscious mind of the receiver and, second, that the intention of the healer is carried by his or her breath and/or words into the herbal pouch. To the recipient, at least, this transforms a simple pouch of herbs into a talisman of real power.

Smudging with Herbs

Smudging is a Native American tradition of blessing, protecting, and sanctifying a person, object, room, or ritual. It is done by placing crushed and dried aromatic herb in a fire-safe vessel, such as a clay pot or seashell, igniting the herb, and wafting the smoke onto whatever is to be blessed. Some herbs with which this can be done are mugwort, sage, rosemary, juniper, cedar, lavender, and sweet grass.

Resinous herbs must be placed on a hot stone or charcoal in order for them to burn and smoke properly. These include the frankincense, myrrh, and copal.

Before an Herbal Tarot reading begins, smudging may be part of the ritual, and some dried herbs may be given to the recipient for smudging at home to further enhance the significance of the reading.

Using Affirmations

Along with the herbal talisman, an affirmation can be given to augment the healing process. An affirmation is a vibrational prayer said over and over again each day so that a more positive and healing energy can be manifested. The repetition of special words causes a particular change, a new resonance, or a restructuring of an attitude to occur. The counsellor may also ask the receiver to take out the charm or talisman and recite aloud and with the fullest possible conviction the affirmation at least five times per day. One should reserve a specific time daily to sit quietly and write the affirmation down in a specially designated notebook. Tremendous power lies in the repetition of a positive word or affirmation but an even greater power lies in writing it. The principle is that action is used to complete the inner thought so that, in the words of the great Sufi mystic, Hazrat Inayat Khan, "when a person thinks, feels, speaks and writes, he has developed the thought through four stages and made it powerful." One will be absolutely amazed at the effectiveness of such a method to help overcome personal blocks, a sense of limitation, or harmful habits. In most cases, events and circumstances seem to align themselves magically, enabling one to move forward with greater ease and peace.

Hazrat Inayat Kahn, in his exemplary clarity of style further states, "As a gift is nothing without the giver, so a charm is nothing without a personality that gives confidence to the patient. Therefore a charm written by an ordinary person has no effect; the personality of the person who writes the charm should be impressive, his/her piety, spirituality, love, and kindness should all help to make the charm that he/she gives valuable and effective."

Herbal Allies

Herbal allies are listed with each herb of the Herbal Tarot. The herbal allies do not have the exact same herbal or energetic properties but they are similar and may be used to further enhance the healing sought. In other words, you are not bound by the herbs on the cards but are free to use other herbs with similar properties that are easily available to you. For example, calming and greater clarity can be evoked by taking a bath with lavender oil or by sleeping on a pillow with mugwort in it. Both are soothing to the nerves and open the mind's eye (sixth chakra; see glossary). These herbs may not be on the cards dealt but their energy may be appropriate for the situation at hand. If you or the person you are giving a reading to is unfamiliar with taking herbs, then it may be easier to get herbal products that are already prepared and have directions with them.

Following Your Intuition

Many times when a card comes up you may look in a book for its meaning. It's fine to do this but sometimes the meaning of the card as written and the situation at hand do not match. For example, a woman was wondering about what new career she could enter. She had been working in a state job for twenty years and as a single mother had supported her son and herself quite well. Now she was able to retire and was looking for a career that would be fulfilling. We had talked at some length about what she enjoyed doing and she mentioned that she had become "mom" to many fatherless boys in the area.

The cards, mainly cups, verified her sensitivity and that the energies she worked with were very healing to others. The last card, however, was the three of swords, whose usual interpretation is emotional upheaval, quarrels, and severing of relationships. Due to the situation at hand, I instinctively knew that this card meant for her to look into a career as a counselor for juveniles and disturbed children "to help mend broken hearts." I recommended some herbs that would strengthen her spiritually for this work, especially in the area of her kidney and bladder, or second chakra. She had a tendency to pull other people's emotions into herself and try to resolve their problems for them. This created some excess in the water element and made her rather water-logged with emotions. The three of swords indicated this to me as well. She needed to cultivate some objectivity or she would experience the pain of others. I recommended meditations, a change of diet, and some herbs that are good for removing excess water from the system (diuretics).

Some situations are very obvious, also. A woman came to see me who was in her early forties. She appeared to be a well-balanced person who was in good shape both spiritually and physically. She felt that her life was great. She had a wonderful marriage, and her kids were doing well. She felt very positive and, as she put it, she was ready to take the big leap into something new and creative. I said, offhand, that it sounded like she was in the "Fool mode." Much to her amazement (and mine), the first card she pulled was The Fool, key 0. We proceeded with the layout, which verified her feelings about taking off into new realms with faith and joyful enthusiasm. From the cards that came up I recommended that she take American ginseng (the Fool's herb) twice a day to give her the energy to move forward and help open her to the inspirations coming. I recommended that she burn sage (V High Priest's herb) to invoke purification, protection, and clarity in her new endeavor. I also recommended an affirmation to help her to realize more fully her strength (VIII Strength) and to let her open up and use her fire quality more comfortably.

So go by your intuitive hits and acknowledge your own knowingness.

The Male/Female Card

We as beings are constantly dealing with the male/female sides of ourselves. Many times a card of the opposite gender of the reader may be taken as representing someone in the environment, but it is also important that we relate the energy to ourselves. Are we using this male or female energy in ourselves in a positive way? How can we create a more balanced and integrated self with the use of this energy? Even if we see this energy in another with whom we are associated, what can we learn about ourselves through this person? To use the tarot as a tool for personal transformation, the cards must be related to the core of our inner being and not just to people and circumstances in the external environment. We can change and evolve ourselves, and through greater inner clarity and peace we can be beacons of light for the world around us.

Behind the Scene:
The Back Design of the Cards

If we look beyond ourselves we will see that the Divine Protecting Spirit is always with us as a guiding light throughout our journey in life. She knows that all our choices are perfect as they will teach us precisely what we need to learn. Her unconditional love is always there to comfort us through our joys and travails.

In the same way, the symbolic design on the back of the Herbal Tarot cards is there to enhance the readings and to remind the seeker that protection and guidance is always present.

The rosemary plant on the back design is in the form of the ancient Greek letter theta θ. The circle divided into two halves signifies spirit–matter held together by the underlying principle of Divine Spirit. Spirit is present in all things that exist. By embracing and perceiving Spirit in all we do, see, and feel, we will be able to go beyond the apparent duality of body and spirit and see that all is one continual Circle of Life. Rosemary has long been used as an herb of purification and protection. If planted at the entrance of a home or garden it is said to impart an aura of protection to the area and to those who are present. If it is used as an incense it will enhance the sacredness of the occasion. When using holy water for anointing and blessing, take a sprig of rosemary and sprinkle the water about with it. The wonderful qualities of this herb will augment any ceremony. Wearing or carrying rosemary will help the seeker and the consultant to be clear of mind and open in heart when the cards are being dealt and read.

The four blue mandala wheels are in the four directions and represent the seasons of our lives—spring, summer, fall, and winter—the beginnings, the growth, the inner values, and the letting go to make way for the new beginning. They also represent the four elements—air, fire, water, and earth—and swords, wands, cups, and pentacles.

The ladybug is a well-known protector of the garden. She will watch over you and see to it that the seeds planted in the readings are allowed to reach their full maturation.

Meditations with the back design on the cards will help to open you to the protection and the guidance that is all around you. Allow intuitive thoughts and ideas to flow through you, for these are part of Spirit's way of communing with her children.

We are never alone on this journey. It is for us to see and feel the fullness of Spirit that is always here.

The Four Elements

All phenomenal existence partakes of the four elements of earth, air, fire, and water. These are not to be confused with the contemporary elements of modern physics but rather describe a broader, dynamic concept in which earth corresponds to the quality of solidity, air to movement, water to fluidity, and fire to warmth and motivation. The traditional four elements have their roots in ancient times and permeated the physical and metaphysical teachings of great civilizations such as ancient India, Tibet, China, the Middle East, Greece, and Rome, as well as the Native American cultures with the medicine wheels and the four directions.

In the European/Western world the elemental system was superseded during the seventeenth century with the teaching of the French philosopher Descartes. Yet there may never have been an attempt to supersede the teachings of the four elements if people had not come to consider the four elements as literal phenomena rather than symbolic metaphors that were and still are useful to describe a broader and more wholistic perspective of life.

Knowledge of the dynamic interaction of the four elements allows us to enter into a deeper understanding of complicated life processes from the level of personal wisdom, observation, and experience rather than from the perspective of rationally known individual facts and pieces of information. Further, the teachings are universal enough to lead the specialist and modern scientist through inductive processes of reasoning to more profound understanding of the physical laws of the universe.

We can all experience the metaphorical, symbolic meaning of earth energy, for instance, as opposed to knowing about a specific mineral with which we are completely unfamiliar. Earth is solid, bulky, supports and upholds life, nourishes, is stable, is a centered point of reference, and so on. These are the qualities meant by the concept of the Earth element.

Air is the opposite. It is cold, moving, subtle, and light. Water is flowing and damp, and it can be converted to steam or ice. Fire is warming, motivating, and vitalizing.

We can understand that all phenomena, including people and animals as well as food and plants, partake to a greater or lesser extent of the four elemental qualities. Perhaps all occult systems, including tarot and astrology, are based upon a fundamental understanding of the energetic qualities of the four elements and, more important, their dynamic transformation and interaction with each other in the eternal dance of life. The tarot, with its four suits and the individual cards of the Major and Minor Arcana, represents a complex symbolic system based upon the four elements of existence.

The ancients intuited that each planet was dominated by one or a combination of the four elements. Human body types as well as individual organs were understood to have predominant one or more of the four elements. Colors, sounds, and emotions were matched with elements, and finally all foods and plants were classified according to the four elements so that they could be intentionally used to restore harmony and health to one in a state of dis-ease and imbalance.

There are three levels of healing: body, mind, and spirit. Physical healing involves using physical manipulations and substances taken internally or applied externally to effect a change in vital physical processes. Mental or emotional healing utilizes counseling to help establish alternative ways of thinking about a situation so that it no longer has a negative effect upon body–mind processes. Spiritual healing goes to the essence of health in that it attempts through the power of thought, suggestion, or ritual to inspire a fundamental understanding of spiritual being and, by so doing, to allow one to make necessary adjustments on mental and physical levels in order to achieve the maximum potential of well-being.

The following essays on the elements will help you to see in a symbolic way how the elements manifest themselves within an individual. You will see how to use the Herbal Tarot deck to bring about a greater balance and healing for those who are seekers.

The Earth Element: Suit of Pentacles
The Earth within Us

Earth is the solid state of matter. Its characteristic attributes are stability, fixity, tenacity (or stubbornness), and rigidity. Spiritually, our earthy part gives inner stability, a sense of values, patience, and groundedness. This element connects us to our bodies, our resources such as our talents or material goods and the solid reality of the world around us. It also gives us a certain feeling of being rooted in the sensuality and "feelingness" of living. When our earth is lacking, we may feel to varying degrees nervous, ungrounded, and insecure. We may also have a hard time making decisions or handling our worldly affairs. On the other end of the spectrum, we may overcompensate in our earth element and find ourselves inert, stuck physically and mentally, unable to move out of fixed conditions, and stubbornly hanging on to our possessions. Mental digestion of experiences and physical digestion of foods may be deficient as well.

The herbs depicted in the pentacles suit assist us in bringing into balance the earth within us and outside of us. This suit includes herbs that affect the physical and spiritual process of nourishment, digestion, assimilation, and elimination. When earth is lacking, it is important to eat the foods and do the things that are nurturing to us. This would include a wholesome diet of grains, legumes, a little meat or seafood (if one is not a vegetarian), and steamed or stir-fried vegetables. Nourishing oneself in this fashion will bring about feelings of well-being and contentment. Creating quiet around the dining table will augment these feelings. Lighting a candle while eating brings focus to the moment and heightens our spiritual receptivity to the food vibrations. Another part of being nurtured is allowing ourselves to love and be loved, to work when we are inspired and to rest when we are tired, and to willingly and lovingly share our abundance, talents, and resources with the world around us.

For those who are too solid and constipated with unresolved life experiences, the bitter herbs, such as gentian, cascara sagrada (cascara bark), and yellow dock root are appropriate. They can help us digest and release the experiences and fixations we may have. Bitters are best taken before a meal to assist in the digestion of foods, or after to relieve heavy, bloated feelings. One teaspoon is usually sufficient.

Some physical and spiritual characteristics of a predominantly earth person are: a solid, large-framed body; slow and steady movements; thick, oily skin and hair; good appetite; loyal in relationships; ability to sleep soundly; conservative use of physical energy and money; greed and attachment to possessions, but if more evolved, generosity.

For those who are either too earthy or lack earthiness, carrying a piece of root from an herb will help in understanding what a healthy internal earth is. Roots are the stabilizing point for plants and much earth energy is stored in them. This energy will be transmitted to the wearer and an improved sense of well-being will be felt.

Respect the earth in you, and around you. It is like a silent, stable mother nourishing and loving you each moment.

The Water Element: Suit of Cups
The Water within Us

Water flows and moves and is wet. It takes the shape of whatever may hold it. It can be a powerful force and yet can appear tranquil and peaceful. Life is supported and created from water. Vast portions of our planet are covered by water, and water makes up over seventy-five percent of our bodies. Within us, water is in the form of our blood, urine, tears, perspiration, saliva, and sexual juices. It lubricates every cell.

Spiritually, the water element can manifest as the flow of thoughts, emotions, and feelings. Water is our ability to be adaptable.

Many times when we have watery dreams and visions, such as looking at the sea, or diving and swimming in the ocean, they are telling us about the balance or imbalance of our watery, emotional self. A water dominant person may have some of the following characteristics: fear of being inundated; feelings of being overwhelmed; water retention in the body; being overly impressionable; overwhelming emotions; penetrating intuition or over-reactiveness to situations; kidney or bladder problems; sensitivity to the needs of others and the tendency to take on other people's emotional upsets. A lack of water can bring about a dried-up feeling; stiffness (emotional and physical); lack of moisture in the body; a non-flowingness with life; difficulty in dealing with emotions and with others who are emotional. A balanced water element is analogous to a clear, flowing river moving in an unimpeded manner.

In the Herbal Tarot, the cups depict the water element. They represent our capacity to have relationships, feelings, emotions, and love. All the herbs in the cups suit work with urinary and reproductive organs, which express the body's watery aspect. These herbs include diuretics, which relieve excess water from the system; male and female urinary tonics; and aphrodisiacs, which help the adrenals. They teach us to be in balance with our watery/emotional selves. They ask us to feel from our hearts and to embrace the Divine Love that always emanates toward us and through us. They ask us to understand that our purpose for being here is to serve ourselves and others with love, compassion, and devotion.

A simple meditation to help the watery self is to put your hands on the second chakra (below the navel) and breathe in deeply and exhale fully. See any cords or energies that are connected to you in this area break away and leave you. After you've done this for a few minutes, move your hands to your heart, breathe deeply and gently, and visualize golden energy flowing all around you. This will help free you from past emotional cords and move you toward the freedom of love found in the heart.

By creating a better rapport and balance with our water within, we will see more clearly that we are not isolated beings but a significant part of the Divine Ocean of Life.

The Fire Element: Suit of Wands
The Fire within Us

What is the fire element? How is it a part of us internally and externally? Fire is warmth, light, liveliness, vitality, and spark. It is the sun who extends his rays to all life. This great solar being is the life-giver who creates a feeling of belonging just as a warm fireplace does in a home. Fire produces change in our lives and brings forth our creative drive. Our internal fire transmutes food and experiences into dynamic power and force. It keeps us warm inside, like an internal sun.

We feel emotional warmth, fired up , enthusiastic, able to move and go. The fire element rules the heart and the circulation. The color associated with fire is red and the season is the hot days of summer. The sound that fire makes in us is laughter and the emotions of fire are joy and happiness.

With a lack of fire we feel cold and uninspired. We have cold hands and feet and poor digestive fires. We may lack warmth in our relationships or are unable to assimilate the essence of our experiences. We may be afraid to express or show our talents, and new situations and projects may intimidate us. On the other hand, there are those who are fire-dominant. They are too hot, too fired up, too aggressive. The fire needs to be tempered. Both situations indicate a fire imbalance. Some characteristics of a fire-dominant individual are: medium build; strong digestive fires but proneness to heartburn; good circulation; aggressiveness, irritability, and jealousy; determination; sharp mind; fiery and angry temperament; passion; impulsiveness. Fire people tend to be self-starters and trailblazers.

The wands suit has the keys that can tell us about our inner fires and how we can best manifest them. The herbs on these cards relate directly to energy and the blood. They include warming stimulants, carminatives (herbs that help relieve gas), and hemostatics (herbs that control bleeding).

Spiritually, they can show us where we need to create more drive and will in our lives or how to temper ourselves so that our fires will not burn us out.

If there is a predominance of wands in a reading then the fire issues can be looked at. Are you bringing out your creative will? Are you open to change? Or are you over-stimulated, aggressive, or competitive? Is there a lack of drive and expressiveness?

Different activities, such as massage, aerobics, dancing, tai chi, and acupressure can bring out or help you to be more in control of your fire element. Affirmations reaffirming your creativity in life can be very effective as well. Meditations with fire or with the sun can be quite illuminating. For sun meditations do not stare into the sun. Sit in the sunlight and consider the virtues of the sun and see how they manifest in you.

Honor the inner fire. Greater health and joy will be yours through a fine tuning with the fire within.

The Air Element: Suit of Swords
The Air within Us

What is the air element and how does it relate to us in body, mind, and spirit? Air is the gaseous, formless state of matter. It is the wind blowing around, moving freely through and amongst things. It is the Breath of Life, *prana*. Without air we stop living. Air is closely associated with our nervous system, the lungs, the mind and thought forms. It is the unifying quality that allows us to adjust to new ideas and different sorts of people and situations. Air is the communion of breath that links all life into one living unit. It can be thought of as the Divine Breath of Life.

In the Herbal Tarot deck, swords designate the air element, the breath, the nervous system, and our minds. They represent the search for truth and are used to sweep away fragments of falsehoods until the whole is finally realized. The swords are the path of trials, conflicts, and struggles unconsciously created by our inner attitudes. All the herbs on the swords cards help to revitalize the nervous system, calm the mind, and open our breath to life, and they help us to maintain a meditative state even through adversity. They include nervines, antispasmodics, expectorants, and calmatives.

Many people in our mind-oriented society are in need of a calm mind and nerves. This is especially true if their air element is out of balance. Some indications of an imbalance are: inability to be steady, whether this be in thoughts or work; excessive talk; fast irregular movement and shakiness; nervous pains; holding one's breath during intense activity; an inability to take a deep breath; living in the head; being out of touch with the body. On the other end of the spectrum, a lack of air may manifest as an inability to take in new thoughts; slow and sluggish thinking; inability to reflect on oneself; difficulty in adjusting to new ideas and people.

People who are air-predominant will have some of the following physical traits as well: dry hair and skin; colder constitution; a tendency to run in high gear and talk in a breathless manner; poor digestion and gas; erratic eating habits and life-styles; extremes in life-styles and ideas; nervous pains and conditions. The life-style that will best sublimate some of these traits includes a regulated schedule; proper rest and relaxation so that the nervous system can regenerate itself; warming and wholesome foods; nervine herbs such as skullcap, and tonic herbs such as ginseng and dong quai; warm baths; meditations and yoga; and more faith that the universe knows what it is doing without our having to figure it all out. It is best to stay away from coffee, black tea, and other stimulants, and it may be helpful to have earth-predominant people nearby to help balance out the air quality.

Air is an elusive but powerful element. If you learn to master it, self-acceptance and a deeper visionary concept of the interconnection of all life will be revealed.

The Major Arcana

0 The Fool

Ginseng; Panax quinquefolium Uranus

0 The Fool

The Fool is our most inner self who is limitless, boundless, adventurous, and immortal. He is guided by his heart's path, symbolized by the rose, and by the divine golden light which he perceives as divine grace pouring down to him.

Because of his innocent trust in the divine, the Fool steps forward fearlessly, oblivious of the impending cliff which will tumble him down through the world of experiences and adventures. In his knapsack he carries those traits and characteristics inherited from his ancestry, previous lives, and cosmic memory. He will use these gifts and powers as needed during his sojourn as an incarnated spirit.

Uranus, an erratic, revolutionary, and eccentric planet, is the ruler of the Fool, thus he may appear to be crazy and outlandish, or creative and original. He is free of self-imposed restrictions and is open to change and inspiration. The Fool, being key 0, is above all of the other twenty-one Major keys, and thus he has freedom of movement. He can appear in our lives when we least expect him. He encourages us to be more detached in the roles that we play and reminds us of our true beingness as children of the Great Spirit. He is a visual representative of the tao or the void, which is nothing and everything. He is our true self, joyously playing the script but never losing contact with the power of life.

Ginseng, Herb of Cosmic Energy

Spiritual properties: In the plant world, ginseng provides pure motivation and creative energy within each person. Its root most resembles an upright human figure and is symbolic of the inner potential each being has when he/she incarnates. Ginseng imparts to us the dynamism that is needed to be a creative, manifested entity. It is like the lightning bolt of the life power.

Medicinal properties: Ginseng can be a powerful building and tonic herb for all weaknesses and lack of energy. It strengthens the lungs, nourishes body fluids, and calms the spirit. Ginseng also increases wisdom, promotes longevity, and builds resistance to disease. There are many types of ginseng, with North American ginseng being milder and safer for general use.

Dose/Preparation: Ginseng herbal essence may be taken as often as needed when the energy of the Fool is being invoked. It will increase the creative energy needed to be an innovative, free spirit. Carry a piece of ginseng and allow the energies of innocence, adventure, and divine guidance to fill you. The herbal essence can be taken as needed for further setting up this vibration within.

For medicinal purposes, a small piece of ginseng root can be chewed on each day. Another way of using it is to simmer a whole root in four cups of boiling water in a non-metallic pan (soluble metals tend to alter the properties of herbs). Use this broth to make a hearty soup with a lean piece of organic meat, some whole grains, and other root vegetables such as potatoes and carrots. Make or purchase ginseng tincture and take one dropperful one or two times a day during the cold winter months.

Key words: Needing or feeling boundless energy. Following one's path with faith. Having an innocent trust in inner guidance. Childlike enthusiasm. Being foolish. Living in the moment. Willing to take chances. Needing to find personal support within.

Affirmation: "I feel the boundless Divine Energy flowing through me. I enthusiastically walk my path in life."

Herbal allies: All types of ginseng, condonopsis.

I The Magician

Astragalus; Astragalus membranicus
Mercury

Astragalus

I The Magician

The Magician represents the power of creative transmutation. He stands in a state of powerful inner attunement, encircled by the golden light of heaven. Upheld in his receptive left hand is a crystal to attract and magnify the pure cosmic energies, while in his lowered, giving right hand he points a finger downward, symbolizing his ability to direct, through concentration, the divine energies into unlimited manifestation.

Around the Magician are strewn the cup, pentacle, sword, and wand, symbols of the four elements of creation and the four suits. The wand symbolizes the fire element, the enthusiasm and energy to make things happen; the cup represents the water element, feelings, and the flow of ideas; the sword represents the air element, the mechanics of how the world works; and the pentacle represents the earth element and the end result of all the above—in other words, the actual physical objects, bodies, and things around us. These are the Magician's tools, which he will master and use in order to make his visions into reality.

Ruled by Mercury, the planet of ideas and communication, the Magician awakens within us the ability to move inward for inspiration and then outward for manifestation. It represents the ongoing communion we have with the creative flow of life. Meditation on this card will unleash the secret of how to develop our power of concentration and the ability to manifest whatever is our true heart's desire. We must always be cognizant, however, that our true power is the Divine Will working through us and we must do our work with a heart that is full of good will toward ourselves and others lest we begin to perform the black arts and get caught in our own web.

Astragalus, Herb of Creativity

Spiritual properties: Astragalus assists in increasing the energy needed to bring about the manifestations desired. It will help bridge any gap there might be between the thought and the creation of the reality. Our ability to digest and assimilate our life experiences will be increased, and any tendency to be "spacy" and ungrounded will be rectified. This herb is a powerful herb of protection and can be used to create a stronger aura around oneself.

Medicinal properties: Astragalus root is traditionally used by the Chinese as a tonic to foster and increase energy by strengthening physical digestion and assimilation. It specifically counteracts tendencies to "spaciness" and ungroundedness so typical in hypoglycemic conditions. It is also the most powerful immune system enhancer known. Since obesity is a condition in which we have lost to some extent our ability to transmute and digest food, just as in the spiritual realm we have lost our ability to transmute ideas, feelings, and experiences, astragalus can be taken regularly to help overcome this tendency.

Dose/Preparation: The herbal essence of astragalus can be taken each day as one is working to awaken the Magician within. A piece of the root may be worn in a pouch to assist one in being a conscious creator in life. Create a Magician's ritual of self-empowerment and make a tea of astragalus as a potion to further imbue the self with the strength to receive and manifest inspirations.

Astragalus is used in teas and soups as described in 0 The Fool. However, the root is much too woody to be chewed directly. It can be made into a tea by simmering four slices of the root in three cups of water for fifteen to forty-five minutes, depending on the strength desired. Three or four Chinese jujube dates, if available, may be added to the tea. One to three cups may be taken per day. Astragalus extract, found at Chinese herb shops, can be taken on a daily basis, or you can make your own alcohol extract and take a dropperful two or three times per day.

Key words: Concentration. Commitment. Magical powers. Communication skills. Writing, speaking. The power to hold your position in time and space and thus create. Manipulating others and their energies. Need to be focused and grounded. Need to see life as a magical manifestation.

Affirmation: "Through concentration and dedication, I am a willing channel of Spirit manifest on Earth."

Herbal allies: Schizandra, asgwaganda (Withania somnifera).

II The High Priestess

II The High Priestess

Peony; Paeonia albiflora
Moon

The High Priestess embodies the pure power of the feminine, receptive principle. She is in touch with the Universal Mind. She has had many names in her past and at one point was none other than the ancient Egyptian goddess Isis, who was able to give life to the god Osiris after his death. Thus, around her neck is the sacred ankh, the key of life. She was also the Virgin Mary, who contained within herself the seed of Spirit to be manifested on earth.

Her left foot rests on the crescent moon symbolizing her dominion of and oneness with inner-reflection and the natural cycles of life. Enthroned between the two pillars of light and dark, she is in a state of silent equilibrium. With a veil over her eyes, she is mute, looking within to the subconscious, in other words, to the consciousness that resides behind all the outer manifestations. She knows there is a Uniting Consciousness behind all aspects of life.

The blue color of her garment and the clouds in the sky are indicative of the watery element over which she reigns. Water is the source of life in that it contains all the thoughts and substances needed for life's expression. Through our own inner High Priestess we are able to tap into our potential creativity and are better able to understand how all aspects of our life are united.

Peony Root, Herb of Inner Knowing

Spiritual properties: Peony root helps to foster and harmonize the feminine energy within. It allows the circulation of our subconscious to flow and move, thus enabling us to get in touch with our essential nature. Through its relaxing, antispasmodic action, a sense of ease permeates one's being as one explores these realms.

A woman who uses this herb on a regular basis will learn how to accept and work with the metamorphosis she goes through from childhood, puberty, motherhood, menopause, and then the wise crone. The beautiful peony flower has a vibration of softness yet deep vitality which is indicative of the basic yin, or feminine, energy from which all of life receives its foundation.

Meditations with the flower or with a picture of the flower can help one to embrace the High Priestess within. Men who are yearning to understand their softer, intuitive sides may partake in this wonderful herb as well.

Medicinal properties: Peony root is commonly used in Chinese herbalism, together with other female herb tonics such as dong quai, false unicorn root, and raspberry leaf, to strengthen those aspects of the blood and female hormones necessary for the monthly cycle, puberty, menopause, and fertility in women. Peony is also used for men and women with hypertension and feelings of anxiety, frustration, and extreme anger, which often accompany cardiac abnormalities. If peony is consumed for a long period of time it is said to add vigor to the body, lengthen life, restore and balance the liver, and make the skin radiant and beautiful.

Dose/Preparation: Carrying a piece of the root in a pouch will remind the wearer to be in tune with their inner knowing. Growing a peony plant in the garden can be very fulfilling as well. Each year in the spring it will renew itself and bring forth beautiful blooms. There are many colors of peony so one may want to decide which one to grow for the color therapy aspect. Choose white for purity of spirit, pink for healing the heart, red for invigorating courage to seek inner visions.

For medicinal uses, four pieces of peony root and one piece of Chinese licorice root may be boiled in two cups of water for fifteen minutes. Drink one cup two times per day. Peony can be purchased from Chinese herb stores. The root slices are white with a very light pinkish hue in them. Many Chinese formulas such as Women's Precious Pills and Planetary Formula's Women's Treasure include peony.

Key words: Exploring the subconscious. Looking for the "why" behind the manifestations. Mystery. Inner knowing. Wisdom. The yin principle of the self. Feminine beauty and grace. Shyness and holding back. Need to let go of tension and nervousness. Paying attention to the cycles of life. Moodiness.

Affirmation: "I open my heart to the answers that lie within me. I see the perfection and unity of all things."

Herbal allies: Rose, hibiscus.

III The Empress

Dong Quai; Angelica sinensis
Venus

III The Empress

The Empress is Mother Nature herself, sitting as the queen of all earthly life. Pregnant, she embodies the fulfillment of the creative impulse in the universe. Behind her flows the clear stream of intuition that is the continuation of the blue gown of the High Priestess. She wears a yellow gown which symbolizes the understanding and intelligence of nature.

The Empress's crown represents the twelve signs of the zodiac and the many expressions of life which they signify. Ruled by Venus, the planet of beauty, harmony, quality, and love, the Empress seeks pleasure and the fulfillment of her heart's desires. Her law is the law of love. She asks us to feel the co-creatorship with the Divine Powers around and within us. She sees no difference between spirit and nature, for she knows that the physical world celebrates the Infinite Divine Spirit.

Dong Quai, Herb of Femininity

Spiritual properties: Dong quai is considered an energy builder for the yin, or feminine, creative energy. It will increase fertility for new inspirations to grow and gives the energy to bring to fruition the creations. In other words, one becomes pregnant with ideas!

Medicinal properties: Dong quai is a very important tonic herb in Chinese medicine. It is renowned for its blood-building and strengthening ability and has been used to regulate the menstrual cycle, aid fertility, relieve cramps, treat all symptoms of menopause, and alleviate anemia. This herb can be taken by men also whenever there are blood and circulatory problems.

Dose/Preparation: A piece of dong quai may be carried in a pouch in order to remind the seeker of the creative river of life of which he/she is co-creator. The herbal essence may be taken as needed. A ritual with the spirit of nature may help to open up the creative flow. Sit on the earth and create a circle all around you. Within the circle put some things that represent the hopes and aspirations you would like to create and embrace in your life. Take three drops of the herbal essence of Dong quai and meditate on the creative energies flowing through you from the Divine Mother.

For medicinal purposes a slice of the root may be added to soups to make a nourishing meal for the family. A tea can be made by adding one root and six jujube dates to three cups of water and letting it simmer down to one cup. Drink one half cup two times per day. It may be combined in a tea with ginseng if there is low energy. Dong quai may also be taken as a tincture or in pill form.

Do not take this herb during menstruation as it may cause excessive bleeding. DONG QUAI SHOULD NOT BE TAKEN BY PREGNANT OR MENSTRUATING WOMEN, AS IT IS A UTERINE STIMULANT.

Key words: Pregnant with ideas. New life and possibilities. Abundance and fruitfulness. Need to pay attention to nature. Need to warm up and to be open to new situation. Compassion and tolerance are in the forefront. Grounding your energies. Create beauty and grace in your everyday life.

Paying attention to the energy and growth of a situation.

Affirmation: "I bring forth my creations with joy. I love and nurture them to fruition."

Herbal allies: Lovage (Levisticum officinale).

IV The Emperor

Atractylodes alba
Aries

IV The Emperor

The Emperor sits on a solid throne, dominating and overseeing all creation. In the distance are the mountains, symbolizing wisdom. His purple garment represents the high consciousness with which he oversees his domain. The blue river in the background is the High Priestess's intuitive wisdom reaching out to him. His left feminine side, facing the viewer, symbolizes the need to balance the strong male qualities which this card suggests with the more feminine qualities of tolerance and compassion.

Ruled by Aries, he is the fiery overlord and the archetypal father who protects and keeps an eye on the things created. The Emperor has in his hand the scepter of the ankh which represents the life force. He uses his internal fire, his logic, and his reason to bring into concrete existence his dreams and visions. Within ourselves he is the yang/male energy who seeks stability and order. He is the mover and shaker who gets things done.

Meditations with this card and the Empress card will help create the balance of the yin/yang energies within.

Atractylodes, Herb of Power

Spiritual properties: Atractylodes is a very warming energy tonic. It will enhance the Emperor inside each of us by giving him the fire and the energy he needs to accomplish his goals. This powerful herb will also help us to digest life experiences and turn them into positive energy for further creations. If the Emperor's energy is used with a lack of wisdom then the herbal essence of dong quai, which is on the Empress card, may be used to help balance the strong, fiery tendencies.

Medicinal properties: Atractylodes is used by Chinese herbalists as a tonic for the spleen and stomach. It is said to help the digestive system and to regulate fluid metabolism. It is often used as a diuretic (gets rid of excess fluid) and to regulate the appetite. It strengthens the muscles and helps to build energy.

Dose/Preparation: Atractylodes may be carried in a pouch to assist in the balancing of the male/father/fires within. The herbal essence may be taken when one needs to hold his/her ground or when one fears bringing one's creations into the light.

Medicinally, atractylodes is used in many Chinese formulas that deal with poor digestion and bloating. The raw root can be made into a tea by itself or combined with ginseng or astragalus to build energy and to increase the digestive powers. When used in conjunction with dong quai, the blood as well as the energy of digestion will be strengthened.

Key words: Power of organization. Divine reason. Protection. Achievement. Difficulty taking in things or ideas. The male within. Putting order in your life. Being too rigid and fixed. Bringing to light one's creations.

Affirmation: "I use my inner wisdom and strength to achieve my goals in life."

Herbal allies: Asafetida, cardamon.

V The High Priest

V The High Priest

Sage; Salvia officinalis
Taurus

The High Priest represents our own inner teacher. After we have come to the end of our reasoning process we must jump into the realm of inner guidance. The High Priest is there waiting for us, for he knows what we need both physically and spiritually and stands as the bridge between the two pillars representing practical and spiritual knowledge.

The High Priest is ruled by Taurus, the sign of inherited talents, values, tenacity, earthiness, and results. The High Priest uses all his Taurean capabilities in order to teach and guide us in a stable and real manner. He is that small voice we hear inside when we take the time to ask the question, silence our minds, and just listen. He is practical in application of wisdom and is willing to live his life according to inner dictates.

Sage, Herb of Sacredness

Spiritual properties: The herb sage comes from the Latin *salvare,* meaning "to save," attesting to its high regard as a powerful healing herb. Various species of sage can be found throughout the world. The herb has been burned in sacred ceremonies of the Native Americans for inner and outer purification. One method of using sage is simply to crumble a few dried sage leaves and burn them in a large sea shell. Waft the smoke on to yourself and around the space that is to be sanctified.

Sage awakens the inner guide and allows a clarity of mind to be present. The sixth chakra is opened and a feeling of greater centeredness is bestowed upon those who use this herb. It aligns group energy into a common vision and for this purpose it can be used as a smudge at the beginning of gatherings and special events.

Medicinal properties: Sage has been used as a tea or mixed as a spice in food to prevent and treat indigestion and gas. It is also useful as a treatment for bladder infections due to its antiseptic properties. It will help in the treatment of colds, flu, and congestion. It can be used externally in the form of a poultice to dissipate bruises and injuries and to promote the healing of wounds. A cup of sage tea relieves mental and muscular tension throughout the body.

Dose/Preparation: For smudging take the dried herb and burn it in a fire-safe receptacle. Carry some of the herb in a pouch and smell the herb whenever you need to have greater clarity of thought or need to be protected and purified in a given situation.

For a tea, take one teaspoon of the herb and let it steep in a cup of boiling water. One cup can be taken warm two or three times a day. This tea will dry up mother's milk and can be taken for that purpose as well. Do not take this herb internally for more than a week.

Key words: Inner guide. Spiritual guidance. Teacher. That which stimulates inner awakening. Following rituals and rules with no inner sense of purpose or meaning. Following a teacher blindly. Guru.

Affirmation: "I open my heart to the channel of wisdom within."

Herbal allies: Mugwort.

VI The Lovers

Parsley; Petroselinum crispum
Gemini

VI The Lovers

The Lovers card, ruled by Gemini, is an expression of the female (yin) and the male (yang) elements within each of us. The female is pointing to the Divine Inspiration represented by the rays of light. The blue river is an extension of the garment from the High Priestess and expresses inner knowingness.

The male is the action, fiery, expressive, and reasoning part of the self. He looks toward his female half to see how the parts of life make up a whole. She is his inner guide and the uniting intelligence. Together, these two parts plus Divine Inspiration create

35

beauty, love and unity in our lives.

Gemini is known as the sign of discrimination, communication, ideas, learning and adaptability. For true communication to be manifested we must be willing to be the receptive listener/receiver, or the yin side, and then become the outward, creative expression of our ideas, or the yang side. The Lovers card asks us to be in rapport with the different parts of the self while seeing how each factor interacts. We are to learn how to be in harmony with apparent polarities. Through loving allowance for others and ourselves we can see and create beauty in our lives.

Parsley, Herb of Discrimination

Spiritual properties: Many times our inner fears cause us to stay closed to the healing of the male or female within us and manifest outside ourselves in the form of difficult relationships. Parsley helps to dissolve those solidified feelings and to allow them to flow out of us. It gives the space for the reconciliation of yin/yang energies. When the Divine Mother and Father are healed within then we can truly feel our internal unity.

Medicinal Properties: Parsley as an herb naturally grows in rocky soils and its roots break up hard rocks just as the herb internally is good for dissolving urinary stones in the bladder and kidneys. It is extremely high in natural vitamin A, making it excellent for the liver and eyes. A tea of parsley can be used to eliminate gas and bloating from the intestines. The seeds and the root of parsley and its near relative, celery, are considered aphrodisiac and are a good treatment for impotence in men.

Dose/Preparation: The herb can be carried in a pouch to remind the wearer of the unity of the yin/yang inside. It will help to loosen up the rigid feelings associated with either gender. The herbal essence will help open the heart so that one can go beyond antagonistic dualities.

Medicinally, parsley can be taken as a tea to help dissolve kidney stones. It can be mixed with equal parts of gravel root, marshmallow root, and dandelion root. One tablespoon of the mixture is steeped in a cup of boiling water for fifteen minutes and three cups are taken per day.

Eating a piece of parsley at the end of a meal will aid digestion and counteract gas.

Key words: Magnetism and attraction. Relationships. Healing the male/female within. Blind lust. Inability to see the other side of an issue. Feeling guilty about a relationship. Cooperation. Need to allow love and beauty into your life. Developing communication and discrimination faculties.

Affirmation: "I feel love and unity within."

Herbal allies: Marshmallow root, asparagus root, celery seeds.

VII The Chariot

VII The Chariot

**Cyperus; Cyperus rotundus
Cancer**

The Chariot is the peaceful warrior who has learned how to harness the energy of his will and is receptive to the inner guidance that is always flowing to him. His body and his personality are symbolized by the chariot. He uses this vehicle during his manifestation here on earth as an expression of his true self. Ruled by Cancer the crab, he is protected against the bombardment of thoughts from the world around him symbolized by the city or the "race consciousness" from which he has separated himself. He is liberated from any old patterns that bind him and has learned to distinguish the true desires of the enlightened self from the compulsive desires of an unawakened self.

Within himself he embodies all the teaching from the first six keys. The celestial symbols on his hat and robe indicate the larger reality that he can now perceive and work with. The blue color denotes the High Priestess's consciousness to which he is connected. He is taking the middle way between the polarities of life, thus he has reconciled the Lovers within. He is learning how to control his moods and emotions by stilling the mind and listening to the inner guide, or the High Priest, and he is using the power of concentration, which is the gift given to him from the Magician. The Emperor has taught him how to organize his activities and rule over his domain and from the Empress he has found the place of peace in his heart. By embracing these gifts he is victorious.

Cyperus, Herb of Regulating Energy

Spiritual properties: Cyperus teaches the way of the middle path. It has the capacity to help regulate energy and is especially useful for those who experience mood swings from joy to depression or energy swings from high activity to no activity. It is a drying herb and so will help to dry up or regulate unneeded emotions/water within. The three-sided stem of cyperus is a signature of this herb's ability to help body/mind/spirit function as a whole rather than in disjointed parts. As can be seen in this card, the charioteer is holding the cyperus which is symbolic of his controlling his energy and will.

Medicinal properties: The root of cyperus was used as a source of food by the Native Americans and is used by the Chinese as an important herb for regulating chi, or bodily energy. Thus, it aids in the regulation of digestion, menstruation, moods, and all natural physical and emotional cycles. It is useful for gas, bloating, and indigestion. For menstrual irregularities it can be taken with other women's herbs such as dong quai and peony. Cyperus is not good for those who are very dry constitutionally or who are wasted due to disease.

CAUTION: THIS HERB IS FORBIDDEN DURING PREGNANCY.

For a decoction, put one ounce of cyperus in one pint boiling water, simmer twenty minutes. Take two to three cups per day.

Key words: Direction from within. Knowledge of inner powers and strengths. Ability to regulate and manifest one's life. Need to filter out group or race thoughts. Need to use one's power towards good will. Need to allow the emotions to be released. Mood swings. Taking the Middle Way. Need to contact the watery part in one's self.

Affirmation: "With my heart as my guide I use my Will and Power to be Victorious in all that I do."

Herbal allies: Poria cocos.

VIII Strength

Cayenne

VIII Strength

Cayenne; Capsicum annum
Leo

By using the strength of love the woman is able to push over the blockages and resistances she encounters within herself and in her life. Leo, the ruler of this card, is the sign of fiery self-expression. The woman wears a red cape symbolizing this energy, and the purple dress represents her inner wisdom which guides her to use her strength in a wise way.

From VII The Chariot, she has learned how to be clear as to what her true desires are and can now direct and control them as opposed to their controlling her. She knows that she cannot employ opposing, brute force to manifest her goals, for this will only bring back to her the same resisting energy. Her internal fires and the healing heart energy are her tools. With the help of the infinite, as symbolized by her figure-eight hat, she knows the path she must take

40

to manifest clearly her creative images.

Cayenne, Herb of Power

Spiritual properties: Cayenne pepper is an herb whose spicy, fiery nature is both stimulating and rallying to the inner resources of power so that one can overcome internal stagnation, blockages, and fears. It has the capacity to open the heart center while allowing one to remain in control of it.

Medicinal properties: Cayenne is a stimulating, warming herb that aids digestion and is primarily useful for all circulatory problems, heart pains, cold extremities, excess mucus, varicose veins, and hemorrhaging. It can also be used to stimulate inner immune reserves to overcome developing colds, flu, and fevers. It serves as a natural stimulant to help overcome tiredness and fatigue and to raise vitality. It is excellent to use for arthritic and rheumatic problems.

Do not take this herb if you are too rundown.

Dose/Preparation: Put a little cayenne in a pouch and feel its warm ethereal energy fill your being. Visualize heat and fire rising up in you and warming your heart. Allow any stagnancy to be melted away and transformed into unresisting love. The herbal essence may be taken during the day when the sun is high in the sky to further augment the power of fire within.

Medicinally, cayenne may be taken in capsule form, two or three "00" capsules per day or as needed.

Key words: Breaking through personal and outer blockages. Courage and strength to face outer challenges. Need to open to inner power and self-love. Need to look at dominating and controlling tendencies. Warming up inner coldness. Strengthening inner vitality.

Affirmation: "I affirm the strength of my heart. My power is one with Divine Spirit."

Herbal allies: Mustard seeds, black pepper.

41

IX The Hermit

Licorice

IX The Hermit

Licorice; Glycyrrhiza glabra
Virgo

The Hermit, ruled by Virgo, is the seeker reflecting on the varied experiences he has had during his long sojourn in life. His consciousness has moved inward and he realizes that the truth he has sought is truly in himself and not in the distractions of the outside world.

The Hermit has learned to help others with love and compassionate detachment. He has gone beyond the point of being critical and is able to see that the varied paths people choose for themselves all lead to the Great Spirit. He no longer needs to convince others of what they should do; for that matter, he does not have to speak very much. He is at a point of needing to be silent and allowing his light to shine. Through his example, those who come in his vicinity may realize that they, too, can shine their lights without fear.

Licorice, Herb of Inner Peace

Spiritual properties: For a very long time licorice root has been used before meditation to help quiet the mind. It opens up blockages in the emotional realm and gently eases them out. In their place will be a deeper sense of peace and understanding. After taking licorice root for a while one will be able to bring into harmony the different parts of oneself or of relations that have seemed out of accord. A greater sense of allowance and harmony will be embraced within.

Medicinal properties: Licorice root, known as the "grandfather of Chinese herbs," is an excellent chi (energy) builder. As a detoxifier it will get rid of poisons due to poor food, alcohol, or other organic poisons. It is a harmonizing agent in many herbal recipes and is used in most Chinese formulas to allow the herbs to work in a more synchronized way. It calms the emotions, moistens the lungs and throat, fortifies the bones and muscles, and detoxifies the blood. Because of its ability to regulate the blood sugar levels it can be very stabilizing for hypoglycemic conditions and for anorexic cases.

Dose/Preparation: Carrying a piece of licorice root on your person will impart a greater sense of peace and harmony. Taking a few drops of the herbal essence will help one to feel detached compassion in situations that may be very turbulent or difficult. Meditations with the Hermit card will help one to see one's inner light.

Medicinally, an herb tea can be made from one or two small slices of licorice root. Put the root pieces in a cup of boiling water and let simmer for five minutes. Licorice root extract can be taken, a dropperful one to three times per day. This herb is not to be taken by those who retain excess water in their system or by those with high blood pressure, as it will exacerbate these conditions.

Key words: Inner seeking. Solitude. Need to be alone. Teaching by example. Having nothing more to say. Need to find peace within. No longer looking outside for the answers. Compassion with detachment. Need to handle quarrelsome situations.

Affirmation: "With patience and inner quietude I follow the guidance of my own inner light."

Herbal allies: Red jujube dates, reishi mushroom.

X Medicine Wheel

X Medicine Wheel

Slippery Elm; Ulmus fulva
Jupiter

The medicine wheel is the Native American's sacred symbol honoring the four directions and the cycles of life. Medicine wheels have been found atop mountain peaks throughout the world, attesting to the universal reverence for this symbol. They are used for prayers and meditations and as symbols for bringing down to earth the sacred power of heaven.

Usually, a large stone representing the Great Spirit is placed in the center. The outer stones represent the four directions and the cycles of the seasons and life. On this card, the slippery elm tree is placed in the center and is used to symbolize the Great Spirit that gives strength, energy, comfort, and nourishment to all.

Ruled by Jupiter, the benevolent planet, the Medicine Wheel card depicts the cycles and turning points in our lives. The medicine wheel asks us to be open to changes and, if we should lose our way, to move back to the center of the wheel where there is stability and spiritual nourishment.

Slippery Elm, Herb of Soothing Nourishment

Spiritual properties: This herb will give the strength, nourishment, and soothing encouragement needed to move through the cycles of life. It softens our resistance to changes and allows us to feel more internal unity and centeredness.

Medicinal properties: Slippery elm can be taken as a tea for irritation of the lungs, throat, and for internal ulcers. It is a highly nutritious food and will stay down even when there is tendency to nausea and vomiting. It is safe enough to give to infants and small children. Externally the powder can be combined with comfrey and/or echinacea with a small amount of cayenne pepper to heal any injury, ulcers, or sores.

Dose/Preparation: Carry slippery elm in a pouch to help you to be open to the flow and changes of life. The herbal essence will enable you to be more at ease and spiritually nourished as a new time unfolds.

Medicinally, slippery elm can be made into a tea. Put a teaspoonful of the powder into a tea bob or bag and let it steep for five or ten minutes. The powder can be mixed with a little water and sweetened to form slippery elm gruel and is a very acceptable life-giving food for seriously ill or recuperating people. A poultice can be made with this herb or a combination of herbs, as stated, for external ulcers and sores.

Key words: Cycles of life. Need to be centered. Faith and trust in the adjusting power of nature which rules all life. Need to focus on goals and aims. Getting a broader perspective. Need to heal. Unity. Need for more devotion and ritual in one's life.

Affirmation: "Through all the changes that Life brings, I feel the center of stability which is within me."

Herbal allies: Irish moss, chickweed.

XI Justice

Plantain; genus Plantago
Libra

Justice emerges out of the dense forest of darkness and confusion holding the crystal of light in one hand and the scales of balance in the other. The displayed sword symbolizes the unqualified search for truth. Her outer cape of red represents strength and power and the inner gown of pink expresses her compassion.

Justice, ruled by Libra, represents our internal need for equilibrium. She is the faithful Divine Mother preserving us and maintaining our health, physically, emotionally, and spiritually. She protects those things which are important to us and with her sword she carves off what is useless and worn out.

Justice is the appreciation and understanding of the laws of nature. When we are in harmony with these laws we are protected in all ways. When we are in disharmony, pain and personal discomfort arise. Justice teaches us how, through work and action, we can cultivate health for body/mind/spirit by being discriminating in the choices we make for ourselves. She wants to take us toward our innermost joy.

Plantain, Herb of Adjustment

Spiritual properties: Just as plantain can remove irritations such as splinters from the body, spiritually, it can help one to identify and clear out inner sources of irritation. Congested thoughts or fixed ways will be loosened up and greater clarity will be created. Through this type of adjustment and re-balancing, a new life can be created.

Medicinal properties: Taken internally, plantain soothes and cools hot inflammation, expels phlegm, and relieves coughing. It helps to restore the rhythmic breath. It is the supreme cleanser and giver of life. It can be used externally for insect bites, bruises, burns, and wounds.

Dose/Preparation: As an herbal essence, plantain may be taken three times a day while saying an appropriate affirmation to enhance the Justice card's energy. A small piece of plantain can be carried as a reminder of the adjustment that is taking place within.

For inflammation or as a diuretic and blood purifier, simmer one teaspoon in a cup of boiling water for ten to fifteen minutes. One cup can be taken three or more times daily as needed. An external poultice can be made by combining plantain and comfrey leaves with a small amount of cayenne pepper as a catalyst. The herbs are steamed or steeped in boiling water for about fifteen minutes and then wrapped in a cloth or applied directly to the injury, wound, or splinter. One can simply chew a leaf of plantain and apply it to the wound.

Key words: Need for better inner balance. Time for work and action. Balancing health habits. Need to discriminate as to what is best for the self. Need to create one's own joy. Taking responsibility for one's actions and relationships. Looking at another side of an issue. Looking at the pros and cons. Need to cut away unnecessary baggage.

Affirmation: "By creating greater balance within, I create more joy in my life."

Herbal allies: Purslane.

XII Suspended Person

XII Suspended Person

A young person hangs upside down in the Divine Ocean of Life. Her/his head and arms form the equilateral triangle known as the water triangle. Her/his usual fiery and exuberant nature in life has been reversed and s/he is still. The hands which govern the outside world are behind the back, for now s/he is working on the inner faculties. The pants are blue, signifying the quieting of the sexual procreative impulses or those impulses that stimulate further endeavors and creations involving the outside world. The green jacket represents healing and rejuvenation within.

The Suspended Person, ruled by Neptune, is learning the art of self-realization and inner quietude in order to go beyond the illusion that we as individuals are the managers of the universe. S/he has a sense of the Divine Wisdom and Essence that guides and unites all the cosmos from molecules to plants, animals, stars, and planets. This concept cannot be grasped in the mind; it is a feeling, a feeling of nonresistance, and a feeling of recognizing the One Essence, the Living Consciousness of the Universe.

48

The Suspended Person is on a vision quest from which s/he is gaining the vision to open up to the unity of the cosmos. Usual thinking must be reversed. This involves moving from escapism to inspiration. S/he sees her/his place in the ever-changing ocean of life and sees that what s/he does in her/his small realm of life is a part of the flow and motion of the Great Divine Sea. S/he realizes that from the state of relaxation s/he can be of service to her/himself and others without the ego stepping in needing praise and approval. S/he is learning to trust in the wisdom of the world, that there is a conscious, wise Presence in and amongst all.

Kelp, Herb of Softening Spiritual Properties

Spiritual properties: The sea vegetable kelp is nourishing, cleansing, and decongesting to the system. The minerals and especially the iodine in sea kelp connect us to the Divine Source of our physical and spiritual existence. When kelp is ingested it pervades the whole system just as the Suspended Person is realizing that the unity of the Divine Life-force is all-pervasive throughout the universe.

Kelp's emollient, softening qualities will metaphorically help to soften the fixed viewpoints and rigidity that the Suspended Person may have. A deeper feeling and harmonizing quality will be embraced in the basic living process.

Medicinal Properties: Kelp soothes irritated throat and mucus membranes, soothes coughs, dissolves firm masses such as tumors, treats enlarged thyroid and swollen and painful testes, and reduces edema (fluid retention in the body or in certain parts of the body). Its high content of minerals is much needed these days due to the lack of minerals in our depleted, chemically fertilized soils.

Dose/Preparation: Kelp can be soaked and cooked in soups or with beans or rolled in Japanese sushi dishes. For those who are not familiar with cooking sea vegetables, kelp tablets can simply be taken with each meal.

To take in the lessons of the Suspended Person, consume some kelp each day and carry a small piece of it in a pouch. Meditate with the card, or if you have the opportunity to go to the ocean, find a piece of kelp or other seaweed while you are there. Feel it with your hands and body and enjoy its smooth, cool touch. Then imagine yourself as the Suspended Person floating with no resistance in the sea of life.

Key words: Faith. Reversal of thinking. Heart above head. Escapism or inspiration. Letting go. Spiritual breakthrough. Looking at things from another viewpoint. Need to relax. Dreaminess. Unreality.

Affirmation: "My heart is a fountain of peace. I bathe myself in Divine Love."

Herbal allies: All sea vegetables, marine algae, bladder wrack.

XIII Death

Elder Flowers

XIII Death

**Elder Flowers; Sambucus nigra
Scorpio**

Death, ruled by Scorpio, is a symbol of rebirth, transformation, change, and initiation. The sun in the background is rising; a new day is being born. The blooming red roses symbolize the rejuvenation that we will experience by shedding our old skin, our old worn-out ways, for the rebirthed self.

Death of the old is necessary for the new to emerge. The old is like the compost heap, full of rich experiences from which new forms emerge. If we resist changes we may experience pain, emotionally and physically, but if we exercise our creative imagination and visualize a new, more peaceful, at-ease self, a self that is in a better position than before, then we can move more easily through the unknown fathoms of death and let it take us from constrictive patterns of the past to emerge like the phoenix soaring upward. Death is getting down to the bare bones. It asks us to look at our true inner yearnings for emotional and spiritual peace. It asks us to be reborn through our union with a Greater Power.

Elder Flowers, Herb of Purification

Spiritual properties: The elderberry bush has for thousands of years been venerated by people of many parts of the world for its magical and medicinal properties. In lore and legend it is an emblem of sorrow and death, because old traditions held the idea that the cross of Calvary was made of a giant elder tree. From that time, the story goes, the elder was never able to grow into a tree but forever remained a bush. In Europe the elder was trimmed into the shape of a cross and planted on new graves. If it blossomed the soul of the deceased person was believed to be happy. In pre-Christian northern Europe the elder was intimately connected to magic and it is said that magic wands were fashioned from the elder branches.

The herb helps to allow the death of the old to be transmuted into the new rebirthed self. It acts as a guardian spirit during the metamorphosis and brings ease as the transition occurs.

Medicinal properties: Elder flowers are used for clearing congestion and putrefaction during the onset of a cold and flu. A tea of the flowers, mixed with equal parts of mint and yarrow blossoms, is an excellent internal cleanser and detoxifier for such conditions. A tea of the flowers combined with an equal part of sassafras is a good remedy for clearing the skin of blemishes and acne.

Dose/Preparation: Make a strong tea by combining one ounce of herb to one pint of water. Steep for ten minutes and drink it as hot as possible. Then go to bed and sweat out the cold or flu during sleep. Elderberry wine has been used in the same way with the addition of a little cinnamon to further promote its diaphoretic (sweat-inducing) capacities. Three cups may be taken per day.

Wearing some elder flowers as an amulet will remind you to be open to changes and to clear out spiritual congestion that may obstruct rebirthing. Take the tea or the herbal essence during the onset of a rebirthing time to allow the old self to be cleansed and the new self to emerge.

Key words: Rebirth. Shedding the old. The end of old relationships. Elimination of outworn habits and things. Renewal. Merging with another or with the cosmos as an expansion of consciousness. Transformation from one form to another. Renewal. Release.

Affirmation: "As the serpent sheds its skin, I renew myself within."

Herbal allies: Linden flowers and leaf, chrysanthemum flowers.

XIV Temperance

Echinacea

XIV Temperance

Echinacea; genus Echinacea
Sagittarius

Temperance, ruled by Sagittarius, is an idealistic and adventurous person. Her blue garment is the yin/watery/intuitive self and the red belt is the yang/fire element of action.

The rising sun shows that a new life is unfolding. Its golden color represents Divine Light and the fire within that lets one dare to honor inner values. The solar emblem on her brow is the sixth chakra opening. She is receptive to the guidance given to her by those beings who are forever vigilant to the needs of the aspirant.

After coming through XIII Death, she is ready to experiment with her new life and is working on balancing the polarities within. Through trial and error and with intuition and logic she will transform energy into artistry. She is the union of the male/female/water/fire.

In her dealing with the public she is learning how to temper herself through cooperation, compatibility, and communication. She is learning to manage her resources, to organize and plan. She is aware of what needs healing and is bringing more balance to those areas.

Echinacea, Herb of Fortification

Spiritual properties: On a spiritual level, echinacea assists in adjusting to changes and in harmonizing polarities. Moreover, the cone top of echinacea creates a spiraling vision if looked at from the top. It is quite mesmerizing, very much like a mandala. This is indicative of the need to recognize the inner steadiness and guidance that is always there for you even amidst the most disagreeable changes and turbulence. Echinacea builds an inner protection against harmful outside influences so that one can meet life with inner strength and steadfastness.

Medicinal properties: Echinacea has been used to clear infections and poisons from the body. It bolsters the surface immune system, aids in the production of white blood cells, and is used for all bacterial and viral inflammations. This is a safe and effective herb that can be used on adults and children. The tincture or the powdered herb can be put on external cuts and infections as well.

Dose/Preparation: For acute ailments a dropperful of the tincture of echinacea or two capsules can be taken every hour or two. The dosage may be lessened after the ailment has subsided, but a small amount of the herb should be continued for a few days after the illness is gone to ensure that a complete healing has occurred. Although echinacea does not destroy friendly bacteria in the intestines, acidophilus capsules, fresh yogurt, or miso may be consumed to maintain the beneficial bacteria that have been lost.

Echinacea gives a peculiar tingling sensation on the tongue. This sensation subsides in a few moments and is just a natural phenomenon of the plant chemistry.

A piece of the root or flower can be carried in a pouch as an amulet to remind oneself of the path of Temperance. A flower essence can be used to help one to be more receptive to the inner guide.

Key words: Idealism. Enthusiasm for new beginnings. Blending of opposites. Experimentation and verification. Inner guide. Managing resources internally and externally. Communication of ideals to others. Self-control. Moderation.

Affirmation: "Through artistry and daring I create new visions for myself."

Herbal allies: Chaparral, honeysuckle flowers.

XV Pan

Lobelia; Lobelia inflata
Capricorn

Lobelia

XV Pan

Pan, ruled by Capricorn, is the goat-man nature god. With his fiery zest for life he frolics and plays in the forest and pastures. He respects nature as the force of all life. The word *pan* means "all." Pan understands nature's rules and restrictions and within her bounds he finds joy and freedom. He asks us to look at our lives and to see the laws of nature with which we are not in harmony. He wants us to realize that the rules of nature apply not only to the external world but to the very core of our inner self as well.

Pan may look like our adversary but he is none other than our innermost self asking us to look at our addictive behaviors, unconscious attachments, and self-imposed limitations. He wants us to get down to the true facts about our lives and not to take ourselves too seriously.

The word "panic" is derived from Pan and means fear and terror caused by Pan. Many times when we see key XV we do panic, but Pan wants us to cultivate a sense of humor and mirth about ourselves. He tells us to laugh and be joyful with our lives. He wants us to lighten up and not take it all too seriously. We truly need Pan to butt us back into balance when we get stuck in our ways.

Lobelia, Herb of Letting Go

Spiritual properties: On a spiritual level, lobelia, ruled by Saturn, can be used as an herbal essence to help us let go of self-imposed limitations. This herb has the capacity to move the stuck chi energy in us and will assist us in finding the inner peace we need in order to face our greatest adversary, ourselves, without panicking. We will learn to lighten up and dance the dance of life.

Medicinal properties: Lobelia has been used to treat asthma, bronchial spasms, and other spasmodic conditions. It helps to open up constrained life chi energy. Used in smoking preparations, it counteracts the desire for tobacco. In large doses it is used as an emetic (induces vomiting) to treat asthma and other mucus-related conditions. When excess mucus is relieved from the system it creates more openness in the lungs and calms spasms. Lobelia should be used as an emetic only under the care of a qualified practitioner.

Dose/Preparation: Lobelia can be used for lung congestion, in small doses, five to fifteen drops of tincture or one gelatin capsule. It may be added to other herb formulas as an antispasmodic. Lobelia can be applied externally in baths, fomentations, poultices, and liniments for muscle spasms. A small amount may be smoked to help break a smoking habit and to treat asthma as well.

Key words: Need to lighten up. Not taking oneself so seriously. Need to break up old patterns. Let go of cares and worries and play more. Spilling out of oneself inappropriately. Hanging on to things that have little truth or reality.

Affirmation: "Laughter resolves all things. I empower the joy within me."

Herbal allies: Pasqueflower, valerian.

XVI The Tower

Garlic; Allium sativum
Mars

XVI The Tower

The Tower, ruled by Mars, represents the inner thoughts and words which we have created to build up a tower of defenses and outmoded ideas. The ego and desires may be the masters rather than the servants of the inner self. In our fortified tower, we have separated ourselves from life and others. Now the lightning bolt of inner awakening has hit us and we come tumbling down from our self-created edifice.

This is a humbling experience to say the least. We are no longer functioning from unconscious egotism or race thought. The Mars energy breaks us out of the inertia of the past. It creates an opening for a new cycle. We can no longer rationalize our old position. We are the dethroned kings and queens who must take a new perspective on ourselves and our relationships. The lightning bolt of inner awakening gets rid of the obstacles.

Garlic, Herb of Breakthroughs

Spiritual properties: On a spiritual level, garlic, ruled by Mars, will cut through most blockages and obstacles we have set up within us. As we go through a Tower experience, we may find that people turn their backs on us or that we are social outcasts, just as garlic with its strong odor can be socially unacceptable. In this alone and humbled state, true meditation and clear thinking can begin. Be willing to take a look at how to approach a situation in a new and fresh way.

Medicinal properties: Garlic is a hot and pungent herb. It stimulates circulation and digestion, counteracts joint pain, clears lung infections, and gets rid of parasites. It activates the immune system and is a preventive in viral and bacterial epidemics.

Dose/Preparation: Three to six cloves of garlic can be taken per day during acute conditions or garlic syrup can be made by pouring one quart of boiling water on one pound of garlic which has been sliced thin. The mix is allowed to stand in a covered vessel for twelve hours. A small amount of vinegar and honey may be added to improve the medicinal quality. One raw clove per day or three to five cloves in an infusion can be taken as a maintenance.

Garlic should not be taken during pregnancy and lactation.

A clove of garlic may be carried in a pouch to invoke strength, purification, and protection.

Key words: Being knocked from a position of arrogance. Being made humble. Preparing the way for true realization. Distress. Crises. Destruction of old ways. New cycle to begin. Cleaning house. Awakening to the truth.

Affirmation: "I inhale and nurture myself. I dissolve the fortress within me. I exhale and cleanse myself. I am open to the awakening within."

Herbal allies: Onions.

XVII The Star

XVII The Star

Skullcap; Scutellaria laterifolia
Aquarius

The Star, ruled by Aquarius, is the key of meditation and hope. The woman's blue garment symbolizes receptivity, inner reflection, and intuition. Her red undergarment and skirt symbolize her vitality and will which is being guided by her inner wisdom. This symbolism is further exemplified by her sitting on the earth, the objective world, while touching into the flowing waters of the inner life that reveals the answers from Divine Spirit.

The lightning bolt that destroyed and humbled the self in XVI has inspired inner seeking. The Tower is now the Star of Inspiration found within our hearts. It is a visitation from Spirit showing the way to understanding the life power, an understanding that is an eternal meditation. To meditate with plants and trees can be very powerful. This type of meditation can show us the gifts and wisdom that are always being communicated to us by our plant brothers and sisters if we but open ourselves to their ways.

Many of our inspirations may come to us as visions, ideas, goals, dreams, or imaginings, but we must quiet the outward, searching mind in order to receive the inner messages. Through meditation we can create a greater peace and stability that will open many doors for us.

Skullcap, Herb of Meditation

Spiritual properties: Skullcap calms the mind and heart and prepares the way to meditation. Its tonic properties will help the inner channel of inspiration to be strengthened so that inner truths can be brought forth and manifested in life. Many times when we have realizations, our bodies and especially our nerves and heart must be prepared to handle the accelerated energy flow. Skullcap seems to have the capacity to strengthen the nerves of the body to receive the inspirations so that they do not create chaos and turbulence in us due to the changes they engender.

Medicinal properties: The herb skullcap relaxes tensions, induces calmness, and counteracts sleeplessness. It eases menstrual tension, strengthens the brain, and is useful in the treatment of epilepsy and seizures. It helps ease and break addictions associated with drug and alcohol.

Dose/Preparation: The herb can be taken as an herbal essence to promote a state of meditative living. All of life can be lived as a conscious experience; by doing so the little things we partake in will bring us greater fulfillment and joy. Carry a small piece of skullcap in a pouch to remind yourself of the star of meditation forever within you.

Medicinally, skullcap, a bitter and cooling herb, can be taken as a tincture, ten to twenty drops as needed. If it is being used to help overcome drug and/or alcohol addiction, put the drops in one half cup of boiling water for half a minute to evaporate the alcohol. The solution is taken when cool. A tea can be made from the fresh or dried herb, but it is quite bitter. Gelatin capsules can be taken as well. Care must be taken that the genuine herb is being sold. Often times the herb germander is sold as skullcap.

Key words: Need for meditation. Time to relax the mind.

Visions. Dreams. Inspiration. Hope. Need to be in the moment. Lack of focus. Discovering the truth within. Renewal. Cleansing. "Spaced out" frame of mind. Addiction.

Affirmation: "With peace and calmness in my heart, I am open to the inspirations that flow within me."

Herbal allies: Rosemary, lavender, lady's slipper.

XVIII The Moon

XVIII The Moon

Lemon Balm; Melissa officinalis
Pisces

The Moon, ruled by Pisces, is in charge of our evolution both physically and spiritually. As we recognize our self-unfoldment, we must confront our hidden fears and the shadow side of ourselves. Our bodies must reflect and incorporate the old and new energies with which we now function.

During sleep, moon energies process the changes that we go through in all aspects of our being: body, mind, and spirit. The Moon also helps us to realize that forces greater than our own thoughts guide our evolution.

The Moon has long been thought of as the Grandmother, the Mother of the Earth. Her reflected sunlight is part of the dreamscape of forms and ideas which are to be and which have been. All things blend in her light and the forms are softened. The primal yin energy that she emanates calls forth in us feelings and emotions that have long been hidden. She is the Piscean mist that sees all things as part of the flowing Divine Life-force. The Moon is the water and the substance of life.

The Scorpion on the Moon card represents the self-centered ego. When the scorpion's internal reality changes, it can step out of its shell and move on to the next form, which is the lizard, a creature with the ability to regenerate itself physically. The rocks represent the mineral kingdom and its evolution, and the plant is a representative of the plant kingdom's evolution. The idea of evolution, metamorphoses, and doing what is instinctive are all part of the Moon's pull.

Lemon Balm, Herb of Evolution

Spiritual properties: The lovely lemon balm, also known as Melissa, has long been known as an herb that balances the feelings and the emotions. It helps resolve moodiness and melancholia. It was sacred to alchemists, and the plant-based philosopher's stone is made from an alchemical preparation of this plant. In a metaphorical sense, Melissa guides us as we traverse the misty emotional state of the Moon and enables us to view our emotions and feelings without getting lost in them. This is an excellent herb for children, who function on Moon energy for the first years of their lives.

Medicinal properties: Lemon balm treats fevers, nervousness, hysteria, insomnia, melancholy, depression, cramps, and gas. It is one of the best herbs for treating most simple, acute children's diseases, not only for its excellent properties but also for its pleasant flavor.

Dose/Preparation: Make a moon tea (as opposed to a sun tea). Place about a half ounce of lemon balm in a quart jar and let it sit in moonlight for two to eight hours. Place the jar on the earth, if possible, so that it can partake in the earth's energy as well. If you need to get in touch with and release deeper emotions, then drink this tea on a full moon night. During the full moon, plants go into a deep meditation and this is a good night for people to meditate as well, especially if they are working on moon energy and past painful emotional incidents.

Medicinally, at the onset of a cold or flu, prepare Melissa as a standard infusion and drink three cups per day.

Key words: Spiritual and physical evolution. Moodiness. Dreaminess. Mystic visions or escapism through emotional and physical addictions. Need to look deeply inward. Paying attention to what your body is telling you. Being pulled toward some purpose. Dealing with the past. Illusions. Feeling alone. Fears.

Affirmation: "My emotions are rivers to the Ocean of Peace. I flow with the rhythm of Life."

Herbal allies: Peppermint, spearmint, catnip.

XIX The Sun

XIX The Sun

**Angelica; Angelica archangelica
Sun**

The Sun's hand rays reach out in a gesture of universal blessing. The ankh represents eternal life, eternal light. The Sun energy loves and illumines all things equally without judgment.

The great solar disk in the sky is a benevolent being bringing warmth, love, clarity, and creativity to the worlds that it touches. This same solar energy flows within us. Our inner Sun asks us to be joyful, light of heart, energized, caring, compassionate, and illuminated.

We are now awakened and, as responsible beings, we are ready to bring form and clarity to the dreams of XVIII The Moon. The Sun represents the full flowering of the self. He asks us to live in the present moment and to experience the wonders inherent in the simplest things we do. It's time to regenerate the self and to follow the heart's path.

Angelica, Herb of Warmth and Compassion

Spiritual properties: Angelica is said to be the herb of angels and to enable one to commune with the angelic realm. It has been used to bring good energy and fortune into one's life. One can partake in the energy of angelica in many ways. As a ritual bath it can strengthen the aura and bring joy to one's essence. When burned as an incense or smudge it gives off a pungent aroma that will help protect and purify the area. It helps open up the heart energy and allows one to traverse the heart's path with more peace and clarity. Wearing angelica as an amulet will remind the wearer of the lessons of the Sun card and will help the wearer to follow the heart's path with faith and certainty.

Medicinal properties: Angelica has been used to improve the circulation, warm the body, and restore strength. It invigorates and warms the stomach, spleen, and intestines. It is also used for congestion of the lungs that is accompanied by thin, white phlegm. It is very useful for cold, rheumatic stiffness.

Dose/Preparation: Meditating on the sun will help one to better understand the qualities that the sun imparts to the universe. Do not stare at our great solar being but rather hold a thought of him in your mind and consider his essence. Carry a piece of the herb in a pouch or meditate with the Sun card. The herbal essence may be taken as needed, preferably around noon, when the sun is high in the sky.

Medicinally, the tea is prepared as an infusion, with a pint of boiled water over a half an ounce of bruised root. Two or three tablespoons may be taken each day, or the tincture may be taken; ten drops two or three times per day.

CAUTION: ANGELICA SHOULD NOT BE USED BY PREGNANT WOMEN, AS IT IS A UTERINE STIMULANT, NOR SHOULD IT BE USED BY PEOPLE WHO HAVE HOT CONDITIONS SUCH AS FEVER, INFECTIONS, OR FEELINGS OF EXCESS WARMTH IN THE BODY. DIABETICS ARE ADVISED NOT TO USE ANGELICA AS IT TENDS TO INCREASE THE SUGAR IN THE BLOOD. If you have any of these conditions, try wearing angelica as a talisman.

Key words: Joy. Creativity. Being responsible for one's creations. Warmth. Following the heart's path. Enjoyment and happiness with life. Living in the moment. Childlike enthusiasm. Openness. Willingness to bring form to one's dreams. Commitment to love. Reaching out. Self-importance. Vanity. Arrogance. Aloofness.

Affirmation: "My heart is one with the Infinite Sun. Compassion and love flow from me."

Herbal allies: Asafetida, lovage.

XX Judgment

Goldenseal

XX Judgment

Goldenseal;
Hydrastis canadensis
Pluto

Judgment, ruled by Pluto, is the full awakening of the inner self. One now knows that s/he is not just a body or a mind but a divine being. This is the resurrection and the reawakening of the true self to a new state and sense of being. The clouds parting represent the things of the mind that are no longer hidden. The horn is Spirit's call awakening us from our unconsciousness. It breathes to us the new life's breath.

The blue water and garment symbolize the flowing consciousness from the High Priestess. Her abilities to see beyond and behind, above and below, are now part of the resurrected self. The outstretched arms show an active receptivity to the ways of Spirit. The golden color in the background is illumination and our inner sun shining through.

It is now time to make responsible choices for ourselves based on the new awareness we have embraced. We must judge how we will best use our new-found energies to create our lives and see where we can best express our talents and abilities. It's time to "walk our talk" and live our inner truths. This is not a time to criticize or to be in judgment of others or the self, but instead is a time to decide what the awakened self can do with the new life that has unfolded.

Goldenseal, Herb of Awakening

Spiritual properties: Goldenseal has the capacity to clear out the old congested ways and make way for the new. Bitter emotions such as grief and astringent emotions such as fear are cleared away and replaced with a purified palate for life.

This powerful herb has the ability to bring clarity as to what our purpose is in being here and can help us confront the fears and misgivings we may have about expressing and living our inner truths. Its pungent smell can help change our inner attitude about ourselves.

Medicinal properties: Goldenseal has been used to remove mucus congestion, reduce inflammation, clear toxins, and restore and strengthen the liver and stomach. This bitter and astringent herb also has the properties of being antibiotic and antiseptic.

Dose/Preparation: Using it as an herbal essence, wearing it as an amulet, or smelling it as in aroma therapy are all useful ways of taking in the healing qualities of goldenseal.

Medicinally, goldenseal is a powerful herb that should not be overused. Two or three capsules a day should be sufficient in treating most conditions such as colds, flu, and infections of all kinds. Prolonged use of this herb in large doses can diminish the favorable bacteria in the intestines that influence the production and assimilation of B vitamins. Taking some miso soup or acidophilus while using goldenseal will minimize any minor negative effects it may have on the good bacteria.

THIS HERB IS NOT TO BE TAKEN BY PREGNANT WOMEN OR BY THOSE WITH HYPERTENSION AS IT IS A UTERINE STIMULANT AND IS HYPERTENSIVE.

Key words: Awakening to the inner truth. Deciding and judging one's actions for the future. New perceptions. Deciding the worth and value of a matter. Seeing one's creative purpose. Time to "walk your talk." Opening up to another dimension of the self and life. Need to wake up to over-indulgence. Craving extremes in pleasure. Atonement.

Affirmation: "The struggle is over. The heart has won. I am reborn. A new day has begun."

Herbal allies: Cinchona bark, barberry.

XXI The World

Comfrey; Symphytum officinalis; Saturn

XXI The World

The World, ruled by Saturn, represents the unity of all the elements and their oneness with Divine Spirit. This card depicts our potential to manifest Spirit on earth.

Saturn has been mistakenly regarded as the malefic planet. A clearer understanding of the planet and its energies will bring greater clarity to the World card. Saturn rules limitations, time, form, and responsibility. It crystallizes thoughts and ideas. It represents the earth plane and all of its wonders.

The four elements represented on The World are the different aspects of creation and the order of the universe: water, or the feelings, inspirations, and balance; fire, the creative, expansive energy; air, the element of wisdom and interconnection of ideas; and earth, or contraction, cohesion, and results. Without this order we as celestial beings would not have the place, space, or time to manifest our visions. These are the tools and media with which we outwardly create the inner visions.

The circle on the card represents the all-encompassing power and energy that was or ever will be. It is the present moment of existence. It is the unindividualized life-force that gains self-conscious awareness through the limitations of time and space and by combining all the elements. When we have reached the consciousness of the World card we are no longer identifying all that we create with the ego or subjective personality. We see our creations as a manifestation of the life-force itself. This plane that we live on is magnificent as it is the place where we can see ourselves through our creations. This extends from the most temporal to the most exalted parts of our lives. If we can see ourselves and the things around us as the life-force manifested, then there is nowhere else that we need to be except right here, right now, dancing to the rhythm of life.

Comfrey, Herb of Unity

Spiritual properties: Comfrey is the herb of seeing the segments and putting them together to create a whole. It helps us to knit our realities and our lives together. Meditations with the herb or the card will enable us to understand better how the world with all its segments is pulled together by the unity of the Divine Creative Energy behind all manifestation. We will see more clearly how to be focused and present so that our visions can be joyfully manifested.

Medicinal properties: Comfrey has a soothing effect upon every organ it contacts. Known as "knit bone," it may be used internally and externally to heal wounds, fractures, sores, and ulcers. It is used for coughs and lung ailments. It helps secrete pepsin and is a general aid to digestion.

Dose/Preparation: Wearing the root or leaf of comfrey in a pouch or taking the herb as an herbal essence will help us to come to a better understanding of how the teaching of the World card can manifest in our lives. When doing meditations with the card, visualize the self joyfully dancing on the beach with the elements of creativity.

Medicinally, the entire comfrey plant can be used, but the leaf is strongest for tissue healing and the root is nourishing.

For wounds, fractures, and ulcers, it is best to use the fresh plant macerated and placed directly on the afflicted area, or made into a warm compress or a poultice. For lung ailments, internal injuries, and bleeding, a decoction is made from the root or an infusion from the leaves. Three cups or more may be taken per day depending on the extent of the illness or injury.

Currently, there is some question about the long-term safety of the use of comfrey. COMFREY SHOULD NOT BE TAKEN DURING PREGNANCY OR BY VERY YOUNG CHILDREN, OR FOR MORE THAN TWO TO THREE WEEKS AT A TIME, as it possibly has toxic effects on the liver.

Key words: Seeing the whole picture. The need for healing. Giving form to Spirit. Uniting the four elements and the four directions. Trying to force a unity before conditions are appropriate. Need to break through inertia and stagnation. Mentally stuck. In a rut. Need for joyful participation in the creation of life.

Affirmation: "I joyfully create my life and see Spirit as the foundation of All."

Herbal allies: Asparagus root, marshmallow root.

The Minor Arcana

Suit of Pentacles

Ace of Pentacles

Whole Grains
Root Power of Earth

Ace of Pentacles

A hand emerging from the clouds lovingly holds the pentacle, the earth element. A pathway leads through the arch which is built with a system of perfect balances and is profoundly strong. The path to living in balance with nature and with the inner self is open to whoever wants to follow it.

We must live our truths—as the Native Americans put it, "walk our talk"—and be cognizant beings right here on the earth. We must seek a balance with our families, our actions, our work, our foods, our bodies, and our words. We must nurture ourselves and accept the nurturing that is available to us on all levels of body/mind/spirit. In reevaluating and letting go of any nonsupportive situations or habits, we may notice that feelings of heaviness and spiritual lassitude will begin to be released. One's desires should not be ignored, nor should one become a slave to them. Work at weeding out desires that are empty and unsubstantial and support those that nourish on a deep level. Just as nature throws her seeds out with desires to expand and flourish, we, too, must be willing to plant our visions, nurture them, and watch them flourish.

Whole Grains

Spiritual and medicinal properties: Whole grains nourish the body/mind/spirit on a deep level. Many times when a person feels hungry or undernourished, grains will satisfy that deep need and longing. If, however, a candy bar or some other type of "empty"-calorie food is ingested, the feelings of being unnurtured and undernourished will persist.

The same principle applies to other activities in our lives. When we are tired we should rest, when we need to exercise we should do so, when we are hungry we should eat wholesome foods, and when we need to give or receive love we should not deny ourselves this gift. We should not be afraid to honor the legitimate needs of body/mind/spirit. However, our desires should be guided by inner wisdom and not by a reactive need that will eventually backfire on us.

Work at being grounded and present. Live in the now of your life and honor yourself in all ways. Abundance flows to you and through you.

Dose/Preparation: When we nourish ourselves on all levels, then we will feel more grounded and centered. When we fill ourselves with "empty" experiences, feelings, or foods, we eventually become lethargic in body/mind/spirit. Carry some whole grains in a pouch to remind you of the nourishment you need and the nurturing ways the earth has. She wants you to be nurtured and nourished on all levels.

Whole grains should be eaten each day. Taken over a period of time they will regulate the energy and build up the inner reserves. They are the basis of sound nutrition and will balance the metabolism of the body. Some whole grains are corn, wheat, rice, buckwheat, and rye. These can be used as a spiritual offering.

Key words: Nurturing the self and others. Taking care of legitimate desires. Evaluating the opportunities that present themselves. Need to eat well, sleep well, and enjoy the fruits of life. Need to get blockages and denials out of the way. Time to create a new balance.

Affirmation: "With wisdom and intuition, I willingly nurture and honor my inner needs and desires."

Herbal allies: All grains.

Two of Pentacles

Yellow Dock; Rumex crispus
Jupiter in Capricorn

Yellow Dock

Two of Pentacles

An islander is dancing on the beach with a lemniscate, symbol of infinity. Her pink gown speaks of her compassion, and the ankh around her neck shows her connection to ever-abounding Spirit. The boats in the background move with the flow of the water and the air. They know how to take advantage of shifts and changes in order to realize continually a new balance.

The islander is learning how to maintain equilibrium through the perpetual changes of life. She knows that through these changes she will be able to have more of her self revealed. As stable and immovable as the physical world appears, it is constantly in a state of flux. Just as the ocean moves all the greenery and sand on the ocean floor, so does the wind, rain, sun, moon, our thoughts and actions change and move the world within which we live. The islander knows that it is important to let go internally and externally those things no longer needed. Weakness and stagnation will result from not using the opportunities that life presents.

Yellow Dock

Spiritual properties: Spiritually, yellow dock will helps to free inner reserves of strength and fortitude. For those who are afraid of change and are stuck in old conditions, it will help clear out some of the old sludge and rebuild a stronger inner self who is not afraid of dancing with life, just as the famous Zorba did even during the most harrowing experiences of his existence.

Medicinal properties: Yellow dock root is used to treat skin diseases, liver disorders, and iron deficiency. It is said to liberate the iron stored in the liver and is used for anemia during pregnancy and for anemia generally. It has a tonic-laxative effect which is good for treating rheumatism and bile congestion and will purify the blood and the whole system. It is specific for a variety of chronic and acute skin diseases, including psoriasis and eczema.

Dose/Preparation: The herbal essence may be taken as needed to reinforce the idea of inner strength and fortitude. It will help one to embrace change as an inevitable part of life. Wear the herb as an amulet and dance to the rhythms of the universe; dance with the eternal changes.

For medicinal use, take two "00" capsules or ten to thirty drops of the tincture three times a day. To take it as a syrup, boil one half pound of the crushed root in two pints of water until the liquid reduces to one half, then add half a pint of blackstrap molasses, which enhances its blood tonic action. Take one or two teaspoons two or three times a day.

Key words: Changes. Movement. Go with the flow. Need to work and dance with the situations at hand.

Affirmation: "I flow and work with the changes and diversity in my life."

Herbal allies: Gentian, Oregon grape root, Ho shou wou, Fo-Ti.

Three of Pentacles

Gentian

Three of Pentacles

Gentian; genus Gentiana
Mars in Capricorn

The master gardener is working with the earth. His fertile fields are all around him. During the waning moon, he harvests the fruits of his labor. His hat forms the infinity sign; he is in tune with the cycles of nature. On his pocket is the Greek letter theta; body, mind, and spirit are working in harmony to create a dynamic power.

The gardener has ideals but he is also a practical man and works with the reality at hand. He is able to handle the mundane and sees it as a part of the steps needed to create his vision. He cooperates with nature and with his co-workers. He can persevere through obstacles and knows that the creative forces work through him. His fiery/earthy nature must harmonize so that he can be not only exuberant but grounded, focused, and patient as well. He must work at assimilating more skills and at cultivating deeper understanding as a foundation for further development of his talents. He knows that he will eventually reap what he sows.

Gentian

Spiritual properties: This herb's cool and bitter energy will help to release excess fires which in turn will allow frustrations and irritations to be released. A smoother flow of energy will occur and a greater degree of digestion and assimilation of skills and understanding will manifest.

Medicinal properties: Gentian is a very bitter tonic for the digestion, liver, and gallbladder. Its most common use is as a digestive bitter with alcohol, taken in small doses before meals. It is also useful in treating hepatitis, jaundice, and most liver disorders.

Dose/Preparation: A flower essence of gentian is used for those who become easily deterred by setbacks. Meditations with this beautiful flower or with a picture of the flower will open the sixth chakra so that a deeper appreciation and insight as to the mechanics of a skill or situation will be revealed and thus one will be able to see their way through a difficulty to a solution. Take the herbal essence or carry a piece of the root in a pouch to help bring out the Master Gardener in you.

For medicinal use, as stated, gentian is taken as a digestive bitter with alcohol before meals. It can be made into a bitter tonic with other bitter herbs and taken in the fall and in the spring as a liver cleanser. A tincture is the easiest form in which to take gentian. Put ten drops in water and take it approximately twenty minutes before meals.

Key words: Acknowledging one's mastery of skills. Harvesting the fruits of the labor. Being focused and grounded. Seeing one's creativity in everyday life. Releasing irritations and frustrations. Reaping what one sows. Willingness to face the realities at hand.

Affirmation: "With consciousness and care I plant the seeds of my life and reap the results of my actions. The challenges and disappointments of my life can be a source of strength and inner growth."

Herbal allies: Wormwood, Oregon grape root.

Four of Pentacles

**Cascara Bark;
Rhamnus purshiana
Sun in Capricorn**

A woman sits on a neat and order-ly checkerboard floor. Her head is covered with a close-fitting scarf and she has a tight look about her. She has reached a place within herself where she feels secure and centered. She understands struc-ture and order and will use these tools to actualize her visions. She is able to reserve and direct her power and will defend her posi-tion when necessary.

Four of Pentacles

The woman must watch that she doesn't get so tight that she become fixated and stubborn. If she begins to think that her power comes from the status she holds or from her possessions then she will begin to function in a fearful way and forget that the true power is Divine Spirit flowing through her. In the background is an outhouse which indicates that she may become spiritually constipated and may need to take a spiritual laxative to loosen up a bit. Immobility and clinging to old things that are no longer need-ed are two areas which need watching. On the other hand, she must take care not to let things pass through without absorbing their full intent and meaning.

Herb: Cascara Bark

Spiritual properties: Spiritually, this herb, also known as cascara sagrada, will enable one to let go of fixed and out-moded thoughts and ideas. Old experiences will be loosened up and released so that there is not a condition of spiritual and mental constipation and toxicity. However, it is also important to absorb the experiences and not let them flow out without taking in their full meaning.

Medicinal properties: The bitter principles of cascara bark stimulate the secretions of the entire digestive system, includ-ing the liver, gallbladder, stomach, and pancreas. It is one of the safest tonic-laxative herbs known and can be used on a daily basis without forming a habit. To prevent griping, anise, caraway, or fennel seeds may be taken at the same time as the cascara when it is used as a laxative. A small dose will have a restoring effect on the liver and the digestive functions, and a larger dose will have a laxative and cleansing effect on the colon, liver, and gallbladder.

Dose/Preparation: To relieve spiritual constipation, carry a piece of the bark in a pouch so that you will more easily release areas of stagnation. The herbal essence may be taken whenever one feels a need to loosen up from fixations. If you need to be reminded of the absorption, centeredness, and sta-bility indicated by the four of pentacles then carry this herb and visualize a strong, centered self in tune with the stability and power within.

For medicinal use as a digestive aid, use a small dose of the tincture before meals, six to ten drops. As a gentle laxative, use twenty drops three times a day. For faster action, increase the dose, using one half to three quarters of a teaspoon of the tinc-ture. Or infuse one teaspoon of the dried and aged bark in a cup of boiling water for ten minutes and drink it before bedtime.

THIS HERB AND ALL LAXATIVES ARE NOT TO BE TAKEN DURING PREGNANCY DUE TO THEIR DOWN-WARD RELEASING ENERGY.

Key words: Stability and security. Creating structure and order. Need to loosen up. Spiritual constipation. Letting go of the old and allowing a space for the new. Fears and anxieties.

Affirmation: "I acknowledge my spiritual power and security. I discover my faith within."

Herbal allies: Triphala, rhubarb root, buckthorn bark.

Five of Pentacles

Five of Pentacles

Mugwort; Artemisia vulgaris
Mercury in Taurus

A woman with crutches sits alone in the cold while people in the village are warm and comfortable in their homes. Either she has consciously chosen to simplify her life or she has had to accept a drastic change in circumstances due to external conditions. Even if these changes are due to external influences she must look inward to see what it is that has needed changing internally.

Most times an unexpected event contains tremendous lessons. The universe wants us to evolve and to become more conscious of our inner stillness within the eternal changes. When we get too stuck in our thoughts and in life, we may unconsciously wish for a change and so the universe provides it. Try not to get stuck in self-pity and regret, for these can be ruthless traps from which it is hard to break free. Have faith that all things that occur are for further enlightenment.

Don't torment yourself about your relationships, money, home life, status, or friends that have left your circle. Look for the light at the end of the tunnel and affirm an inner faith as a new day unfolds.

Mugwort

Spiritual properties: Spiritually, this pungent herb has been used for "smudging," the Native American practice of burning herbs for protection and purification. It has been called a visionary herb, as it seems to give one a clearer view of life, and it imparts a deeper sense of peace. Dream pillows are made from mugwort, and the aroma from this herb will augment the dream state and help one to remember it.

Medicinal properties: Mugwort is a very bitter digestive tonic. It is an excellent nervine for uncontrollable shaking, nervousness, and insomnia. The Native Americans used it to treat colds, flu, and bronchitis, and it was taken hot for sweating therapy. Mugwort will bring on the menstrual cycle and can be mixed with cramp bark to treat menstrual cramps. Internally and externally, it is an effective remedy and preventative for parasites and worms.

Dose/Preparation: For smudging, take dried mugwort and burn it in a fire-safe receptacle such as a clay vessel or a shell. The smoke is used to purify oneself and the environment. A ceremony or prayer circle is enhanced with the use of this wonderful herb. While the changes indicated by the five of pentacles are being made, be still and ask for help and guidance. Carrying some of this herb in a pouch and smelling it during the day will help maintain a more calm and clear perspective of the present moment.

For medicinal use as a tea, take half an ounce of the herb and steep it in a pint of boiling water for ten minutes. The dose is one teaspoon diluted in water taken three times daily. Mix ten drops of the tincture into some water to dilute its strong taste and take before meals to facilitate digestion.

DO NOT USE MUGWORT INTERNALLY WHEN PREGNANT. It has an emmenagogue effect and can cause miscarriage. It can be used as a smudge, however.

Key words: Letting go of the old. Making way for changes to occur. Freedom from the restrictions of the past. Taking the bitter lessons life gives. Cleaning out the old. A new day is dawning. Simplicity. Worry and concern.

Affirmation: "I see the richness in my spirit and acknowledge my inner values."

Herbal allies: Motherwort, wormwood.

Six of Pentacles

Hops; Humulus lupulus
Moon in Taurus

Six of Pentacles

The man sitting on the earth is holding a bag full of prosperity—money, talents, information, compassion, or energy. This prosperity is being shared between himself and another, for whatever one gives will be received in kind. The city in the background is the society within which he works and symbolizes the cooperation by individuals that is needed to make a caring and compassionate group.

Through patience and perseverance goals can be achieved, and through openness and mutual receptivity whatever is needed will come. Look for opportunities to share what you have and be open to what others want to share with you. Guard against giving and receiving in a way that is ego-oriented. When you do not feel good about the exchange, then don't make it. Giving and receiving must be from the heart to be of benefit to either party. Any tendencies to go to extremes with this energy must be watched for, such as, giving when there is no need or request, thus experiencing depleted energy or resentment. Look to the heart for the answers, for there you will know that true giving/receiving comes from Divine Spirit.

Hops

Spiritual properties: Hops flowers have been used in dream pillows to induce a peaceful sleep. Make a small pillow case and stuff it with hops and sew shut the open end. Other herbs, such as lavender, chamomile, and mugwort may be added. Place the pillow near your head when you go to bed and have pleasant dreams. Hops will benefit one who is closed off to either giving or receiving. Its flowers worn in a pouch will remind one to be open to the inflow and outflow of the universe. Just as the tides ebb and flow so we must also be emptied before we are filled again.

Medicinal properties: Hops is used to treat insomnia, nervous tension, anxiety, restlessness, headache, and indigestion. It is much used as an aromatic bitter in alcoholic beverages, such as beer. It will calm, reduce pain, and induce rest. It is used for delayed and scanty menses due to estrogen deficiencies. Its bitter taste will enliven the appetite and cleanse the liver, spleen, and digestive system.

Dose/Preparation: As stated, a dream pillow may be made with hops, and the herbal essence may be employed during times of nervousness and/or when one has fears of loss or a lack of receptivity. A deeper faith will be set up so that there will be an openness to allow the universe to provide for our needs both great and small. For medicinal use, hops can be made into a standard infusion or a tincture may be taken. Hops over six months old are not very effective and actually may have a stimulating effect.

HOPS SHOULD NOT BE USED DURING PREGNANCY.

Key words: Willingness to give and receive. Giving from the heart and not the ego. Creating greater harmony in groups. Cooperative attitude.

Affirmation: "I open myself to the abundance of the Universe. I am a channel for her expression."

Herbal allies: Rosemary, lavender, skullcap.

Seven of Pentacles

Seven of Pentacles

Rhubarb;
Rheum palmatum
Saturn in Taurus

With his hoe in hand, a young man sits reflecting on his past efforts and considering the work ahead. Whether or not his past expectations were fulfilled, he must plan to open up new avenues of work which may be more satisfying to him on all levels of body / mind / spirit.

There is hard work ahead and now is the time to gather the discipline and the strength necessary to move on to the next step in life. New fields need to be plowed, the weeds pulled, and the seeds planted.

However, the man must watch that he does not become so rigid or caught up in setbacks that he is inflexible and stubborn. On the other hand, he must guard himself from being undisciplined. Fears, failures, and worries connected to past and future efforts must not paralyze him to the point that nothing gets done.

Rhubarb

Spiritual properties: Spiritually, rhubarb will assist in tuning in to the earth and the inner joy of creating on this planet. Constipated feelings and congested creative flows will be opened up and let loose. For those who are letting their energy dissipate without form, rhubarb will help to staunch this undisciplined flow and encourage direction of the energy toward fruitful results.

Medicinal properties: Rhubarb root is one of the best herbs for treating diarrhea and dysentery by *clearing* the cause of the intestinal irritations. With its astringent action it will staunch diarrhea and watery stools. In small doses, it aids digestion and is an effective tonic for the stomach and other digestive organs. When chewed, it stimulates the flow of saliva. It may be taken alone or added to other formulas when the symptoms of constipation are present.

Dose/Preparation: Carrying a piece of rhubarb root will help to implement the energy inherent in the seven of pentacles. Taking a few drops of the herbal essence whenever one feels stuck or unfocused will be of great assistance. Acknowledge your failures and successes, for both have served as great teachers for you.

Medicinally, rhubarb root can be taken as a powder in gelatin capsules, one to three capsules each time, depending on the use (three capsules for a laxative effect). The tincture is taken in teaspoon quantities, up to a tablespoon for the treatment of amoebic dysentary. When using rhubarb root, it may be a good idea to take a little ginger root to help prevent griping. If you should make a tea from rhubarb root, do not boil it, lest its laxative effect be lost.

DO NOT USE RHUBARB DURING PREGNANCY.

Key words: Need to get working. No time to sit on laurels.

Feeling immobilized by fear of failure. Learning from past experiences.

Affirmation: "I look at the past and learn how I can now create a better tomorrow."

Herbal allies: Senna, aloe.

Eight of Pentacles

Eight of Pentacles

Ginger; Zingiber officinale
Sun in Virgo

With tools on hand, the craftsman looks carefully at his work. He has learned his skill well but knows that there is always more to learn and to perfect. The practice of good self-discipline assists him in making the right choices. Financially, he is aware of how to keep the books balanced, and physically, he has been learning how to keep himself in good health for he knows that these are some of the resources he must rely on in order to keep going in life.

The need to establish strong foundations and roots so that an expansion can occur is imperative. Making the proper preparations and creating the time and place to create is part of the craftsman's understanding.

What he must watch for is that he does not get caught up in idle pursuits or get so lost in the details that he forgets to look at the whole picture. Taking care of the body's needs is important, also, for proper rest and nutrition is part of the healthy, creative flow.

Ginger

Spiritual properties: In the past, ginger was worn as an amulet to bring health and to protect the wearer. It was also used to attract money toward oneself. This plant can help one to become motivated, get the energy moving to use talents in constructive ways. The inner craftsperson will emerge, and any feelings of stagnancy will be eliminated. The juices will really begin to flow.

Medicinal properties: Ginger gets the blood moving and warms up the body. Because of these qualities it is considered a stimulant. It is of great benefit to the stomach and intestines and is used for indigestion, cramps, and nausea. It can be applied externally to treat pain, inflammation, and stiff joints.

Dose/Preparation: The herbal essence can be employed to generate the creative impulse, for when this card comes up it is time to get busy and practice skills no matter what they are. Self-criticism and judgment are not needed now. A willingness to work and to be very present with the details of the moment must be sought.

Carrying a piece of ginger in a pouch will get the dynamic fires of creativity to flow and will dissipate stagnancy and the unwillingness to use skills due to a self-critical attitude.

Medicinally, ginger tea, made by adding two or three small slices of fresh ginger to a pint of water and simmering it for ten minutes, is used for indigestion, cramps, and nausea. Taken with honey and lemon it is an excellent treatment for colds and flu and will help to sweat out the illness (stimulating diaphoretic).

Externally, a cotton cloth soaked in ginger tea and applied to a painful or inflamed area will help to relieve the symptoms. Keep changing the cloth to keep a constant warm temperature on the skin. The skin should become red as the circulation increases.

Use with care during early pregnancy and use only small amounts, a tablespoon per dose, any time nausea or vomiting occurs.

Key words: Being prepared. Learning and creating with your skills. Being orderly with your time and space. Keeping books balanced. Maintaining a physical balance with resources.

Affirmation: "I work in a meditative and steady way in order to create the results that I desire."

Herbal allies: Black pepper, cayenne, galangal.

Nine of Pentacles

Dark Grapes

Nine of Pentacles

**Dark Grapes; Vitis viniferae
Venus in Virgo**

A prosperous woman looks at and touches some plump grapes. She is fully enjoying the harvest from her past efforts. Although she experiences great pleasure, she is very discriminating as to how she spends her time, money, and energy. She didn't get where she is today with frivolous spending and wastefulness. Her great love and passion for her work, whether she is a householder or an executive, has given her a deep sense of peace and security within.

91

Avaricious tendencies must be guarded against and she must watch that she does not become envious of other's situations or belongings. If she should become discouraged because her goals have not yet been attained then she may need to reevaluate her aims and focus more on the creative process than on the end results or rewards. She must not invalidate or be unwilling to accept the praise or support that she may receive from the world around her for this may be some of the prosperity coming towards her. "Abundantly" is the way that the universe functions. We are not meant to close ourselves off from whatever abundance nature provides.

Dark Grapes

Spiritual properties: Grapes have been written about metaphorically in ancient books and its virtues extolled. In the Song of Solomon it is written, "Let us get up early to the vineyard; let us see if the vine flourish, whether the tender grapes appear...there will I give thee my loves." The grapevine has borne the fruit of prosperity and abundance since the beginning of its time. To pull out a bottle of wine is to celebrate the joy of life or at least our joyful participation in its sorrows. When this card is prominent in a session the part of the herb that best suits the situation can be used: the root to invoke abundance; the leaf to clear the heat of envy, selfishness, and dissatisfaction; the fruit to fully acknowledge the harvest.

Medicinal properties: Grapes are a nutritive tonic herb that treats deficiencies of the blood and energy. The root may be used for strengthening the blood, as it is high in iron, and the leaves are used as an astringent and a mild alterative (blood purifier) for inflammatory conditions. It also treats thirst, palpitations, rheumatic and joint pains, difficult urination, and edema.

Dose/Preparation: An herbal essence of the leaf or root may be taken in accordance with the energy to be emphasized. Making a prayer or an affirmation wreath out of grape vines and decorating it with symbols of the abundance which you have or wish to have in your life can be not only fun but very illuminating as well.

Medicinally, fresh grapes and juice are highly nutritious and may be taken on a daily basis. A standard infusion of the leaves may be made and taken three times a day. The roots, which are high in iron, may be decocted and taken three times per day as needed. Cheers and prosperity to you!

Key words: Enjoying the harvest. Discrimination in choices. Tendency to be greedy. Need to be open to abundance.

Affirmation: "I am open to the abundance that my labor and talents provide."

Herbal allies: Raspberries, dong quai, vitex.

Ten of Pentacles

Ten of Pentacles

Wild Yam; Dioscorea villosa
Mercury in Virgo

The ten pentacles climbing up the card indicate the multitude of inner virtues, values, skills, talents, established conditions, inheritance, or material possessions that have accumulated and are available for use. There is a sense of consolidation of past experiences and an opening for new opportunities from this foundation. The house in the background indicates stability, solidity, belonging, and comfort.

When one has talents or a wealth of inner values and virtues, it is important to share and utilize these tools in some form of service to the community around you. By being willing to show the world your talents, whatever they may be, you can be assured that there will be a return flow. For those who have accumulated wealth in one form or another, it is important not to become fearful of losing it all. One can get caught in boredom or apathy because one sees that goals have been accomplished. However, one is never limited by talents, just by judgments. So work at creating and using the gifts that you were born with or that are bestowed upon you on this journey.

Wild Yam

Spiritual properties: Spiritually, just as this root draws into itself concentrated energy from very deep in the earth, it will reveal accumulated energy and power. Through its releasing action it will encourage the use of talents, gifts, and possessions for the greatest good. For those who are fearful of losing their possessions, wild yam will help gently release this inhibition and allow new creative energies to flow.

Medicinal properties: Wild yam root is a valuable antispasmodic for treating bowel spasms, hiccoughs, menstrual cramps, and muscle pain. It is used in the treatment of arthritis and inflammations of joints. As a bile stimulant it treats colic and is useful in the correction of intestinal gas. Large doses are emetic (induces vomiting).

Dose/Preparation: The root of the wild yam may be carried in a pouch or taken as an herbal essence to enhance the ability to accept joyfully the fullness and the completion of cycles within oneself.

This herb may help one to see that inner will can be aligned to the Divine Will and thus see the creative impulse and the accompanying prosperity as a spiritual manifestation.

Medicinally, wild yam is used in small quantities, as an ingredient in herb tea formulas or in capsules taken twice daily. It is a good assisting herb in glandular balancing formulas as well as in liver formulas.

Key words: Sharing talents and skills with the community. Alignment of one's will with spirit. Prosperity. Consciousness of the resources available. Need to loosen up on possessions. Acknowledging one's values.

Affirmation: "I feel the abundance of my life and fully embrace it."

Herbal allies: Black haw, cramp bark.

Page of Pentacles

Page of Pentacles

Blue Flag; Iris versicolor
Earth of Earth

The page is looking for new knowledge and skills. She is ready to learn how to use the tools on hand so that she can plant the seeds for future growth. She wants to understand the earth within her as well as the earth upon which she lives. She listens and takes into herself the messages and visions the earth may reveal. Willingly, she takes the risks that may be necessary as she embarks on her present opportunity. The child within is asking to come out in order to experience the excitement and curiosity of this new possibility.

The page must not to be shallow in her endeavors or reckless in learning her new skills. She must strive to work hard and in an orderly way so that she creates a good foundation for the future harvest. She needs to have faith to go forward and not hold herself back because of fear that she is not capable enough for the job.

Blue Flag

Spiritual properties: Blue flag gets the creative juices flowing and allows any stuck energies to be released. Meditations with the beautiful flower will bring inspirations to the forefront and open up the internal channel of creativity. It will diffuse frustrations connected to the creative flow and diminish thoughts of inadequacy.

Medicinal properties: Blue flag purifies the blood, is diuretic (releases excess water from the system), cholagogue (promotes the flow of bile), and laxative. The root is used for all chronic and acute liver disorders. In large doses blue flag can cause nausea and vomiting.

Dose/Preparation: The herbal essence may be taken when there is a need to open up to the energy of the page of pentacles within. The smell of the iris is very soothing and can be used in aroma therapy. In the spring when the energy for creativity is in the forefront and the irises are in full bloom, make a bouquet of them and allow the aroma to fill the air.

Medicinally, the tincture of the root may be taken ten to twenty drops per dose three times per day or one or two "00" capsules per dose. Blue flag may irritate the digestion in some people so it should be closely monitored.

Key words: Listening to the messages from within about your creativity and skills. Messages from the Great Earth Mother. Opportunity to learn a new skill. Reconsidering values. Taking risks physically, financially. Need to be orderly. Watch for wastefulness of energy and resources. Faith that the seeds planted will sprout.

Affirmation: "I am open to the new skills and creative endeavors that are being revealed to me."

Herbal allies: Milk thistle, dandelion.

Knight of Pentacles

Elecampane; Inula helenum
Air of Earth

Knight of Pentacles

The knight of pentacles is a stable, reliable, and loyal person. Because of his understanding of the healing arts and the ways of the physical world, he is able to teach his wisdom through his actions, accomplishments, and words. His patience is symbolized by the snail-like helmet that he wears. His brown coloring indicates the earthly realm with which he works closely. He knows what it is to be rested and relaxed and recognizes that these activities contribute to greater health and well-being, and clearer thinking. As a businessman he is quick of mind, analytical and industrious and is able to bring his endeavors to success.

He must watch not to be overcritical of other's shortcomings or jealous of their accomplishments. He must work on healing himself first and thus by his example he will be an effective teacher of the healing ways of the earth. Stagnation, inertia, and holding back energy, such as physical energy, talents, or money, will cause a blockage in his system which will eventually need releasing.

Elecampane

Spiritual properties: Elecampane will help one to be more connected to the earth and to appreciate the elegance, strength, and beauty of oneself and others. This herb's pungent taste will get energy moving and its bitter taste will clear away outmoded ideas and fixations.

Medicinal properties: Elecampane is rejuvenative tonic for the lungs. It is used for chronic cold lung conditions with clear expectoration, cough, bronchitis, and asthma. It strengthens digestion, assists in assimilation of food, and inhibits the formation of mucus from weak digestion.

Dose/Preparation: The herbal essence may be taken when there is a need to incorporate into oneself the healing energies of this knight or when these energies have been blocked. Chewing on a small piece will also be effective. Its pungent, bitter, and earthy taste will help one to be more conscious of the clearing, moving, and grounded energy that is needed at this time. The third eye will be awakened and will create a clearer perception. Medicinally, a standard decoction may be made from the root, or the tincture may be taken at a dose of one half teaspoon. For chronic lung ailments it can be combined with wild cherry bark, comfrey root, and licorice.

ELECAMPANE IS CONTRAINDICATED DURING PREGNANCY DUE TO ITS UTERINE STIMULATING NATURE.

Key words: Loyalty. Steadfastness and reliability. Working as a teacher or teaching by example. Need to get moving. Creating the vision and following it. Paying attention to your body's needs. Carrying out the need to ground ideas.

Affirmation: "By being in tune with Mother Earth, I strengthen and heal myself."

Herbal allies: Cardamon, thyme.

Queen of Pentacles

Marshmallow

Queen of Pentacles

Marshmallow;
Althaea officinalis
Water of Earth

The queen of pentacles is a sensuous woman who is very much in touch with the earth and physical life. She knows how to nurture and care for herself and others. Her pink head covering is representative of her compassion; her red garment shows she is willing to get in touch with physical resources and put them to use. She has the ability to be focused and direct in getting things done. She is the personified Earth Mother and wants to see, feel, touch, and smell life. If advice is needed she is the Wise Woman to consult.

However, she must watch that she does not interfere with others' choices or think that she knows what is best, otherwise she will feel drained, empty, ungrounded, and uncertain about her nurturing role. She must learn how to carry through with her primary responsibilities and when to let go of situations that are out of her control. By observing nature she will see what it means to be a faithful and loving nurturer.

Marshmallow

Spiritual properties: Marshmallow root can be used as a means to alleviate grief, fear, and other harsh emotions. It will assist in replacing them with softness, love, and compassion.

For those whose healing work has left them with a drained feeling, this herb will do much to rebuild inner strength. Be careful not to take into yourself other people's upsets and emotions. Doing so may deplete the second chakra area and the kidneys.

Medicinal properties: Marshmallow root is a highly nutritive tonic herb. Its softening and emollient qualities are due to its high content of mucilage. It allays inflammations, soothes the mucus membranes, and cleanses and rebuilds the kidneys and the lungs. For lung ailments it can be combined with such herbs as elecampane, comfrey, and licorice or can be added to kidney/diuretic formulas to harmonize the action. It can be used for ulcers, difficult or painful urination, cough, and tuberculosis.

Dose/Preparation: Using the herbal essence each day will metamorphose anger or excessive sympathy into inner softness and compassion from the heart. A piece of marshmallow root may be chewed to augment this process. It will give a sense of greater connection to the sensuousness of life and help one to feel one's roots within Mother Earth.

Medicinally, a standard decoction may be made from the root and one cup taken three times a day during conditions of inflammation. A poultice can be made from marshmallow to relieve external inflammation, infection, and ulcers.

Key words: Need to be nurtured and to nurture. To be in the body and enjoy the touch, sights, tastes, smells. Being practical in dealings. Someone to turn to for advice. Cultivating greater respect for the earth, your body, and the food that nurtures you.

Affirmation: "I feel the joy of being on the earth. I am nurtured and nurture others with my bliss."

Herbal allies: Aloe, rehmannia.

King of Pentacles

King of Pentacles

Alfalfa; Medicago sativa
Fire of Earth

The king of pentacles is seated on a throne of rock and is looking directly at the viewer. His robe of red indicates his ability to confront and deal directly with the needs and requirements of living on the earth. Patience, willpower, and understanding of how the world works are his talents. He knows the body is a temple for spirit and sees the material world as the stage for spiritual growth. He works to achieve stability in finances, health, emotions, and in his home. He is goal-oriented and reaches for the heights of success.

The king must watch that he doesn't get so fixed on his goals, achievements, and rewards that he forgets the Spirit behind material manifestations and thus becomes stubborn, selfish, resistant to change, and overly focused on material security.

Alfalfa

Spiritual properties: Alfalfa helps one to assimilate nutrients and material treasures. It helps us discover that which is of true worth and value, which coincides with herbal lore that attributes to alfalfa the spiritual power to remove anxieties about money. Taking alfalfa helps us to see our talents and worldly accomplishments as tools for our spiritual reflections rather than as reasons to become more fixed and rigid.

Medicinal properties: Alfalfa is used to help in the assimilation of protein, calcium, and other nutrients. Its cooling properties makes it useful in reducing fevers and joint inflammations. Alfalfa is very beneficial to the blood, acting as a blood purifier and as a remedy for arthritis and anemia. It includes an abundance of minerals and vitamins and is very high in chlorophyll.

Dose/Preparation: Carrying some alfalfa in a pouch will help both in the assimilation of and the reception of those qualities and tangible objects that have real value. From such a place of inner security, we can remain stable and grounded without being fixated on past achievements. The herbal essence may be taken as needed to achieve this result as well.

Fresh alfalfa leaves can be eaten in soups, salads, or as a steamed vegetable. A tea can be made using one or two teaspoons of dried alfalfa per cup of boiled water. Steep for ten minutes. The regular use of alfalfa will help normalize body weight, but, according to the Chinese, excessive use will cause one to lose weight and become thin.

Key words: Mastery of the workings of the world. Goals. Achievement. Management of finances and values. Being grounded and responsible for one's earthly existence. Seeing the earth as the forum for spiritual growth. Stubbornness. Resistance to change. Worries about security.

Affirmation: "I work with the earth and all her gifts to see more clearly the manifestation of my spiritual self."

Herbal allies: Nettles, dandelion leaf.

SUIT OF CUPS

Ace of Cups

Ace of Cups

Lotus; Nelumbo nucifera
Root Power of Water

A chalice overflowing with divine love offered from the hand of the Great Spirit is greeted by the dove of peace. The lotus, symbol of divine love, inner peace, and enlightenment, blooms upon the peaceful sea of the mind.

Listening to and following the heart's wisdom is the focal point of the ace of cups. When we listen to our heart's song we can know our true hopes and desires. The heart is the middle path between our thoughts and our unconscious demands. It "knows" without having to figure it all out. When we move to the heart's path we find deeper inner peace and divine grace bestowed upon us. Devotion, faith, and dedication to Spirit are all manifested in us when the path of love is acknowledged in our lives.

Lotus

Spiritual properties: The lotus symbolizes purity and peace. It is revered not only for its intrinsic beauty but for the evocative symbolism of its growth. The lotus grows in shallow ponds and lakes, its roots extending into the mud where, in the darkness and murkiness, it is nurtured by the earth. As it reaches for the light above, it emerges and blossoms into a glorious exaltation of life. The lotus helps us to embrace our own true inner self with a loving respect. Greater serenity and peace fills us as we move into lotus flower consciousness.

Medicinal properties: Nearly all parts of the lotus have a use. The leaf is taken as a tea to treat fevers, irritability, excessive sweating, scanty urine, diarrhea, and dysentery. The seeds are used as a nutritive tonic as well as a medicine for phlegm, catarrh, and inflammation of the eyes. The nodes of the root also have nutritive astringent properties and are used to treat many forms of bleeding and hemorrhaging. The root proper has similar but weaker properties and is commonly used in Asian cuisine as a tonic food. Finally, the plumule, which is the sprout that grows out of the seed, is used to lower fevers and quiet and calm excessive mental activity.

Dose/Preparation: The herbal essence may be taken throughout the day three drops at a time to foster love for others and the Divine. The seeds can be strung and worn as an amulet or carried on the person as a talisman for peace and serenity. The seeds are a specific for opening the heart center and the roots are used for the opening of the root center (first chakra).

Medicinally, the herb can be taken as a decoction, or in powder form in capsules, or as a food.

Key words: Following the heart. Faith and hope that the light will be revealed. Need to calm the thoughts. Feeling one's deep connections to Mother Earth and Father Sky. Devotion. Visions of aspiration.

Affirmation: "With pure devotion, I open myself to the wisdom of my heart."

Herbal allies: Hibiscus flowers, chrysanthemum flowers.

Two of Cups

Two of Cups

Uva Ursi; Arctostaphylos uva ursi
Venus in Cancer

A man and a woman face each other as equals. The caduceus between them indicates that theirs is a healing relationship. The cups are filled with the accumulated experiences of their wisdom and knowledge. The card represents the highest possible union of two souls becoming one.

Here we are made aware of the need of becoming strong within one's self before forming an intimate relationship with another. While such strength can be found within a relationship, the process is frequently made complicated by the disadvantages of co-dependency. This imbalance between two souls is often expressed in increased conflict and stress, necessitating more individual work on issues of self-esteem.

Uva Ursi

Spiritual properties: Uva ursi, the Sacred Herb of Mt. Shasta, symbolizes the purifying stream of love. We actualize our love energy when it flows to another through intentional acts of caring. Uva ursi clears blockages and irritations one feels toward another and thereby awakens one to the divine presence in all.

Medicinal properties: The herb serves to cleanse and purify the genitourinary tract. Thus it is most often used to treat bladder and urinary tract infections as well as to help normalize blood pressure by regulating fluid metabolism. It is also helpful in regulating blood sugar, making it useful for the management and treatment of certain types of diabetes.

Dose/Preparation: The leaves and berries can be worn as a love talisman and the essence can be taken three times daily to awaken one to the healing lessons indicated by this card. Manzanita may be substituted for uva ursi as it is in the same genus and has similar but somewhat harsher properties.

Medicinally, a standard infusion is made by pouring boiling water over the leaves and steeping the mix until it is cool enough to drink. One cup is taken three times per day. This herb should not be boiled, otherwise it will lose its potency.

Key words: Relationship. Harmonious union. Combining strengths. Coming together. Acceptance of another. Focusing on positive qualities rather than differences.

Affirmation: "I recognize the spiritual strength and power that is created from our union."

Herbal allies: Pipsissewa, manzanita.

Three of Cups

Three of Cups

Trillium; Trillium pendulum
Mercury in Cancer

In a wooded clearing we behold a mythic scene. Three muses dance in life-affirming joy. Here life celebrates itself. There can be no greater tribute to life, no greater reason for living, than the joy of pure being. If the purpose of life is the attainment of mystical God awareness, such awareness comes closest in moments of unconditional love, self-acceptance, peace, and the pure joy and happiness depicted on this card.

The artist, symbolized by the brunette in purple, celebrates the joy of others. The golden-haired one in red salutes the dance of life, and the brown-haired lady honors the glory and power inherent in the growth of the herb.

As the herb seems to arise spontaneously out of love in the loneliness of the dark woods, we are, through grace, given the inspiration of joyous affirmation. Such an awareness is never earned through conscious seeking or determination because it is in the very spontaneity of the moment that all possibilities arise.

Trillium

Spiritual properties: Trillium represents that quality within each of us which imparts value in life. It symbolizes all that we are inclined to nurture and protect. It fosters within us our ability to give birth to spontaneous joy with life.

Medicinal properties: Trillium, sometimes called bethroot or birthroot, is so named because of its favorable influence upon the birth process. It has general tonic properties while at the same time promoting general relaxation of the pelvic nerves. Its astringent properties help prevent miscarriage and excessive loss of blood.

Besides its benefit during pregnancy, it has considerable value in controlling all forms of uterine hemorrhages and discharge. It is best used both internally as a tea, powder, or tincture and externally as a douche or suppository. External treatment is best taken once or twice daily.

Dose/Preparation: Take the herbal essence three times per day and visualize yourself in a joyful participation with life. Be like the devas of the woods and dance your dance. Carry a piece of the root to invoke this energy as well.

Trillium, along with lady's slipper, should not be harvested from the wild because of dangers of over-harvesting. Cultivated varieties are available and preferred for the sake of ecological concerns.

Generally, a standard decoction of the herb is given using a teaspoon of the dried and cut rhizome. A low-potency tincture of approximately five to thirty drops at a time is also effective. The herb may be taken three times per day.

Key words: Joy. Celebration. Friendship. Dance of life. Guard against taking things too seriously.

Affirmation: "With joy, I embrace and welcome all that I have fostered and created."

Herbal allies: Black haw, squawvine.

Four of Cups

Four of Cups

Burdock; Arctium lappa
Moon in Cancer

A woman watching the stream of life appears satiated and disinterested in the offering of the four cups before her. Sometimes it seems that despite achieving all the rewards of friendship, family, and children, something yet is missing. It may be difficult to feel connected with what is happening in the outer world when we feel disconnected from the self within. Nothing is lost if we allow a few opportunities and experiences to pass us by. Allow the flowing stream to carry with it random thoughts and ideas until it eventually runs clear.

Perhaps it is time to contemplate those things which are of more lasting value. Or might it not be time to remain alert and take notice of the further opportunities that life may offer? Don't overlook the gifts offered to you. Be grateful for the smallest blessing in your life.

Burdock

Spiritual properties: Burdock root offers many opportunities for healing. It will help the emotions and watery self to flow more freely while nurturing the self to be more content and stable. Anger, aggression, bias, and excess ambition will be relieved. Stagnation or discontent with what one has or is will begin to clear up and be transformed into more positive perspectives.

Medicinal properties: Burdock root, also called gobo, has blood-strengthening properties and can be used as a blood and lymphatic purifier. It exerts its main influence as a diuretic for the urinary system and skin.

Burdock root and seeds are a near specific for skin ailments such as eruptions of pimples, acne, boils, and sties. It is also very useful for a variety of urinary problems, especially frequent urination and urinary inflammation. Serving as a cleanser of the blood and lymphatic system, burdock is indicated for most joint pains and to help eliminate tumors.

Dose/Preparation: The root can be worn as an amulet to invoke the feelings of being nurtured and cleansed of stagnation. The seeds can release anger and resentment, and the prickly flower heads can remind one to not take life too seriously. The herbal essence may be taken three times per day.

Medicinally, the root can be sauteed alone or with carrots and seaweed in sesame oil, and served as a delicious root vegetable with meals. It can be simmered for twenty minutes using approximately an ounce of the dried root to two cups of water. The seeds have even more specific components in them for clearing the skin. Approximately one tablespoon of crushed burdock seeds are steeped in a covered cup of boiling water to make a tea. One cup of either the root or seed tea should be taken three times per day for best results.

Key words: Need to see what is being offered. Discontentment and apathy. Time to meditate. Seeing the true value in one's life. Finding inner peace and contentment.

Affirmation: "I am open to the blessings that come my way and find inner contentment each day."

Herbal allies: Dandelion root and leaves.

Five of Cups

Horsetail

Five of Cups

Horsetail; Equisetum arvense
Mars in Scorpio

On a gloomy, cloudy day a man sits despondently "crying over spilt milk" or the things he has lost from his life. The loss may be in the form of divorce, separation from a loved one, or general depression.

Under circumstances of grieving it may not occur to him to focus on assets, indicated by the cups standing. The card serves as a reminder against over-indulgence in negative thoughts and feelings. We are midway on the ten-fold path of cups and changes are flowing our way. Sometimes this card indicates the need to reevaluate one's life and perhaps restructure priorities. If this is achieved, then there are possibilities to begin a new unfoldment into a more positive direction.

Horsetail

Spiritual properties: Horsetail helps to clear out fiery emotions that are suppressed by feelings of loss or depression. It gives one the clarity of vision needed during the trying times indicated by the five of cups. Hidden survival instincts will be stimulated and grief will be alleviated.

Medicinal properties: Horsetail, an ancient plant that has been found in fossils from ages past, removes excess water from the system (diuretic) and purifies the blood. Only the barren stems are used medicinally. They appear after the fruiting stems have died down. They have the appearance of hollow stalks and are used either fresh or dried; as with most herbs, they are most efficacious when used fresh.

Horsetail is used for urinary stones, kidney afflictions, blood in the urine, or spitting of blood. It is also used as a remedy for nighttime urination. It is used internally and externally as an eyewash for various inflammatory eye conditions such as pink eye, redness, pain, clouding, blurred vision, and excessive tearing.

Dose/Preparation: As a talisman or herbal essence, horsetail can be worn to put one in touch with primal survival instincts and to give one the strength and endurance needed to get through any internal and external blockages.

For medicinal uses, make a standard infusion using an ounce of the dried or fresh herb to a pint of boiling water. Allow to steep until cool enough to drink. Strain through a cloth carefully for use as an eyewash.

Key words: Focus on the gifts that remain rather than on what has been lost. Despondency. Suppressed anger at losses. Need to see the brighter side. Delays. Emotional transitions.

Affirmation: "From my losses I gain the experience to create a brighter tomorrow."

Herbal allies: Agrimony, cornsilk.

Six of Cups

Six of Cups

Watermelon; Citrullus vulgaris
Sun in Scorpio

Two children play at love. The boy, bedecked in roses symbolizing desires of the heart, is making an offering of watermelon to the girl who is standing in attentive detachment. This card shows a need to touch in with childlike innocence of loving and add more playtime to one's life. At this stage of a relationship, there is no serious commitment; to achieve this, both partners will have to be willing to scale the lofty peaks of commitment for a deeper bond.

Emotional immaturity and toying with another's feelings are to be watched for. These can only create a feeling of instability and eventual betrayal.

Watermelon

Spiritual properties: Watermelon is a food that reminds one of hot summer days and taking time out to enjoy the fruits of the earth. When we eat a slice of watermelon we have to get our face and fingers into the food just as we did when we were young. The child inside comes out. The energy of watermelon is cooling and will temper any excess heat of aggression and anger.

Medicinal properties: Watermelon is used as a cooling refrigerant in hot weather. It is useful to give when there are symptoms of heat stroke and associated thirst. The seeds are used

114

for all urinary affections including scanty urine, fluid retention, edema, blood in the urine, bladder and kidney inflammations, and urinary stones.

Dose/Preparation: The seeds may be carried in a pouch or the
fruit eaten during the warmer seasons to foster the quality of
playful light-heartedness, or to help avoid overseriousness.

For medicinal purposes, simmer or steep a tablespoon of
the crushed seeds in a cup of boiling water for fifteen or twenty minutes. Take three cups daily.

Key words: Innocence. Not taking the emotions of another
seriously. Playing. The child inside. Friendship. Sharing in a
loving way.

Affirmation: "Lovingly I give and lovingly I receive the gifts
of our friendship."

Herbal allies: Melon seeds generally, cucumber seeds.

Seven of Cups

Juniper Berries

Seven of Cups

Juniper Berries; Juniperus communis
Venus in Scorpio

All things are possible! A key idea of this card is self-love, which arises from the power gained from the awareness of self-confidence. Possibly, one may indulge in self-aggrandizement, the inclination to consider oneself superior to others. In any case, at this stage we recognize the inner state of our being reflected in the outer world. With this recognition we may choose the path of adeptship as we seek to understand what is being reflected back to us from others, or we can become emotionally stagnant, overindulgent in pleasures or vices, or caught in our illusions of how things are supposed to be.

The seven cups arranged in an upward spiral symbolize the seven chakras. The science of yoga assigns a specific power or energy to each of these centers. With the awakening of these powers comes a sense of one's true purpose.

The snake represents the seat of kundalini or life energy (first chakra); the smiling mask is the emotional center (second chakra); the jewels are the center of energy and power (third chakra); the red castle is the house where the soul resides (fourth chakra); the bay leaf wreath is the orator's headdress and the ability to communicate thoughts (fifth chakra); the heart bridges the path of the mind with the heart

116

path (sixth chakra); and the blue dragon is the releasing of the self to the divine expression of life (seventh chakra).

Juniper Berries

Spiritual properties: Juniper berries are said to purify the aura and to protect from negative thought forms and influences. As each of the chakra centers becomes more open and more invigorated, juniper berries will help channel the energy toward the highest good for the self and others. Fantasies and unreal expectations and actual needs will be clarified.

Medicinal properties: Juniper is a diuretic (removes excess water from the system) and is also used as a carminative to aid digestion and assimilation. It has a decidedly spicy and warm energy that aids in appreciation and assimilation of food. It is generally considered useful for noninflammatory urinary disorders and has been used with considerable success for general urinary infections. It is useful along with goldenseal to help regulate blood sugar levels and as a treatment for diabetes.

Dose/Preparation: Juniper berries have a wonderful pine fragrance and can be used in aroma therapy to reinforce the positive lessons of this card. They will bring clarity to thoughts and purify the aura. The berries can also be carried in a pouch or worn near the chakra that one wishes to strengthen. The essence can be taken three times per day.

Medicinally, one tablespoon of the crushed berries are steeped in a covered cup of boiling water for twenty minutes or until cool enough to drink. Take a cup two or three times daily. Do not boil the berries or their volatile oils will dissipate. The tincture is taken as a carminative to prevent and eliminate gas and bloating. It is also used in treating urinary disorders. Juniper berries may be taken in combination with other herbs that deal with the urinary and kidney systems.

JUNIPER BERRIES ARE CONTRAINDICATED DURING PREGNANCY.

Key words: Possibilities. Realizations of inner powers and capacities. Watch for overindulgence. Fantasies.

Affirmation: "I recognize myself as I am reflected in the outer world."

Herbal allies: Buchu leaves, cornus berries, cedar berries.

Eight of Cups

Eight of Cups

Gravel Root; Eupatorium purpureum
Saturn in Pisces

A person is embarking on a journey into the night. The moment has come when one realizes that further progress can take place only after the lessons have been carried deep into the mysterious night of the subconscious. Such moments can appear to be a retreat or escape, though on closer examination they are a way to coalesce one's powers. The card is under the influence of the waxing moon, signifying growth and expansion. Do not be afraid to leave old emotional baggage behind but realize the perfection in the lessons learned. New shores await you.

Gravel Root

Spiritual properties: Gravel root helps to loosen up solidified emotions and feelings and allows them to be free-flowing and fluid. A sense of relief will be felt as this begins to occur.

Medicinal properties: Gravel root relieves excess water from the body and is a tonic to the kidneys and bladder. If there is frequent or nighttime urination, gravel root will diminish the frequency of urination while increasing the volume. It is commonly taken to help dissolve and expel stones from the urinary tract. For such conditions it is best combined with a quarter part marshmallow root to soothe the accompanying irritation. As a genitourinary tonic it is useful for impotence, sterility, and inflammation of the prostrate.

Dose/Preparation: To enhance the process of loosening up stuck and solidified emotions, take the herbal essence or carry some of the root in a pouch as a talisman. Visualize yourself in the boat depicted on the card and feel the joy and hope moving within you as you leave the old shores and make way for new lands.

For medicinal purposes, make a standard decoction using approximately two tablespoons of the herb to two cups of water and gently boil it, covered, for about twenty minutes. Take three cups per day. If the tincture is used, take thirty to sixty drops three times per day.

Key words: Leaving old emotions behind. Moving deeply inward to reevaluate the emotional situation. New shores are waiting.

Affirmation: "I acknowledge past emotions and make way for the new, rejuvenated self to be revealed."

Herbal allies: Parsley root, marshmallow root.

Nine of Cups

Nine of Cups

Squawvine; Mitchella repens
Jupiter in Pisces

A woman sits in an attitude of self-satisfaction. She may be ready to give birth to a child or, because of her accomplishments, she may feel a sense of complete personal fulfillment. Three plumes in her hat symbolize achievements.

The snowy mountain peaks in the background indicate that this is only one of the steps along the way and that there are yet mountains to climb to realize one's potential. Give yourself a pat on the back but don't get so complacent and lazy that you stop creating. Share your love and joy with others and allow your inner light and expression to flow from you.

Squawvine

Spiritual properties: This herb will inspire self-confidence, especially regarding the capacity to share oneself physically with another. There will be a feeling of a greater connection with the Mother Earth and an inner acknowledgment of the fruitfulness and abundance that she provides for her children.

Medicinal properties: Squawvine, also known as partridge-berry, is commonly used as a womb strengthener and as an aid in facilitating childbirth. It is useful in relieving menstrual irregularities as well as promoting fertility and protecting against miscarriage. It has soothing diuretic properties which make it useful in both men and women for the treatment of urinary inflammation with accompanying pain and possibly bleeding.

Dose/Preparation: The herb can be worn as a talisman or taken as an essence to inspire the seeker to greater acceptance of the abundance in life. Meditations with the card will help one to focus on and acknowledge personal accomplishments.

Medicinally, a standard infusion can be made, using one ounce of the herb to a pint of boiling water, covered until cool enough to drink. Take one cup two or three times daily or take the tincture, ten to thirty drops, three times per day. This is a good herb to take toward the end of pregnancy to help ease birth pains.

Key words: Self-satisfaction. Achievement. Self-acceptance. Giving birth to the dream.

Affirmation: "I share my visions and feelings with those to whom I am close."

Herbal allies: False unicorn root, pipsissewa.

Ten of Cups

Ten of Cups

Marijuana; Cannabis sativa
Mars in Pisces

The ten cups are precariously balanced as an inverted triangle on an unstable watery foundation. Around and behind, clouds and a rainbow further signify passing illusions. This may be a time for celebrating the rewards of life but do not lose yourself in the celebration to the point of uncentered intoxication.

Learn to maintain inner equilibrium just as in an old Chinese text it states, "in their pleasures and joys they were dignified and tranquil." In this way one can see and be conscious of the energies that are connected to the emotion of joy.

We can learn life's lessons through joyfulness and bliss and not, as it is so often thought, only through pain and grief. Be open for new insights and fresh states of awareness, but don't get lost in "the pie in the sky" syndrome. Be suspicious of the possibility of ungrounded delusions.

Marijuana

Spiritual properties: There is always danger in taking oneself too seriously. Joyful intoxication can be used as an exercise to learn to discriminate the true inner reality from outer delusions. In one sense, intoxication is at the heart of all living. Through insight and meditation on the moment at hand, one

122

can pierce the illusion that can veil the eternal truth and reality of existence.

Medicinal properties: Marijuana is used for relieving eye problems associated with nervousness. These include various eye opacities including glaucoma and cataracts. The seeds, which carry none of the hypnotic properties of the leaves and the flowers, are also very useful as a demulcent (softening) laxative. As such they are crushed and used for constipation in much the same manner as psyllium seeds. Topically, marijuana leaves can be steamed and directly applied as a poultice to relieve arthritic and rheumatic pains.

Smoking marijuana gives a feeling of temporary euphoria and marijuana has been used by dying people to help with the transition. Habitual use of marijuana will weaken the kidneys, and one's motivation and drive may be diminished. Thus, it may hamper one's ability to carry out plans and responsibilities.

To help cleanse psychedelic drugs from the liver and brain and to strengthen the adrenals, the East Indian herb calamus can be used on a daily basis, in the form of tincture or capsules, or in a tea.

Dose/Preparation: Although the use of marijuana is against the law in most states, one must use personal discretion as to whether or not to partake in the use of the herb. One may simply want to carry a few seeds in a pouch as a reminder of the need to accept the happiness and joy in life and not to be fixed on the things that are not "quite right." Meditation on the inner meaning of the card may help us to invoke this vision as well. The essence gives one the opening to live life with inner quietude, peace, and joy.

Key words: Blissful feelings. Nurture and acknowledge those experiences where joy is found. More negatively, delusion, indolence, and unrealistic fantasies may be suggested. It may be time to release mental fixations and examine in a new light the implication of the burden of assumed responsibilities. Carrying out plans and responsibilities. Inability to be grounded or real.

Affirmation: "I take full responsibility for the creation of my immediate reality."

Herbal allies: Poppy, peyote.

Page of Cups

Damiana; Turnera diffusa
Earth of Water

Page of Cups

A youthful, androgynous figure sits on the banks of a stream which symbolizes the subconscious and inner emotions. S/he is fishing for something new in his/her life and is dipping into the emotional stream of consciousness to get a feel for what may be coming his/her way.

There is a yearning for love, new adventures, and intimate relationships. Fresh, youthful enthusiasm and a willingness to take chances are necessary. Be watchful of your dreams and intuition. Look for opportunities to serve others in a joyful, loving way.

The page must guard against flippant superficiality in relationships, lest she or he drown in turbulent waters.

Damiana

Spiritual properties: This herb symbolizes freedom from self-consciousness in relationships. With greater self-confidence comes social attractiveness.

Medicinal properties: Damiana is a mild herbal aphrodisiac and affects mainly the kidneys and adrenals, which are the seat of sexual power. It is useful for both male impotence and female frigidity. It is also useful for male prostate weakness as well as symptoms associated with cloudy urine.

Dose/Preparation: Damiana berries may be worn as a love charm or to attract the type of relationship one desires. The herbal essence can be taken freely to help support the page's quality of liveliness and enthusiasm.

Medicinally, the herb is taken in the form of a powder or extract. Ten to thirty drops is a therapeutic dose. A tea may also be made by steeping a teaspoon of the dried herb in a cup of hot water. Cover it and let it steep for about fifteen minutes or until it is cool. The tincture or the tea may be taken up to three times each day as needed.

Key words: Youthful enthusiasm in the pursuit of new relationships. Sexual interest and desires. Jumping into situations without being responsible for one's actions. Feelings of emotional obsession or dependency toward another.

Affirmation: "I am open to new loving relationships."

Herbal allies: Fo-ti, saw palmetto.

Knight of Cups

Sarsaparilla

Knight of Cups

Sarsaparilla; Smilax officinalis
Air of Water

The knight of cups is the active, airy aspect of the water element within each of us. He is on a tireless search for identity in relationship to another. His winged hat suggests the spirit of a self-styled crusader or messenger of the gods. He has a dream and he is actively in pursuit of it. He is unafraid to express his feelings, tastes, and visions to others.

On the positive side he can represent a stage leading to deeper personal commitments, but on the negative side, he may lose, if only temporarily, a sense of personal identity through getting caught up in the turbulence of immature relationships. He must guard against moodiness and jealousy.

Sarsaparilla

Spiritual properties: Sarsaparilla symbolizes purification of the emotions and the associated ability to express clearly our most intimate thoughts and feelings with others.

Medicinal properties: This herb has an unsubstantiated reputation of increasing sexual potency. It is not always easy to determine, however, why a plant affects people in certain ways. Sarsaparilla is primarily used as a blood and liver purifier. Other specific uses for it include the treatment of rashes such as eczema, psoriasis, and acne. It is also good for individuals whose digestion is weak, with bloating, rumbling, and fermentation.

Dose/Preparation: Use the herbal essence to foster physical and emotional clarity. The herb may be worn in a pouch to foster courage in manifesting openness and clarity in expressing feelings and intentions. Smelling the herb will help in this way.

Make a standard decoction, simmering one half ounce of the root in a pint of water for ten minutes, or make a sun tea with the root. It has a very delicious flavor not unlike root beer. It combines well with other herbs including sassafras, burdock, and dandelion root, which complement its therapeutic effects.

Key words: Awareness of opportunities for sharing intimate thoughts, ideals, and feelings. Renewed commitment to deepening love and intimacy with another. Making love a creative experience that is shared with another.

Affirmation: "I create opportunities to share my thoughts and feelings with others."

Herbal allies: Dandelion root, red clover, barberry root.

Queen of Cups

Lady's Mantle;
Alchemilla vulgaris
Water of Water

The queen sits on a rock surrounded by the sea of emotions and yet is close to the shore of earth representing a centering and grounding of the emotions. To further strengthen this symbolism, she is situated behind lady's mantle, an herb whose main function is to coalesce the water (emotions) and earth (manifestation) elements within.

Queen of Cups

The queen of cups represents a woman in full command of her powers of visions and dreams. She knows what she has to offer and what she is capable of receiving. She is not lost in hopeless romantic delusions but like the moon she is able to reflect to others what they most need to see in themselves. She loves the ocean or large bodies of water and is inspired and healed by their proximity.

Our queen definitely chooses not to indulge in feelings of loss or deprivation in affairs of the heart, but she should watch that she does not indulge in extreme mood changes, thereby deceiving herself and others as to the precise nature of her real feelings.

Lady's Mantle

Spiritual properties: This herb symbolizes the power of control, especially over the emotions relating to others. It can therefore help overcome an excessive dependency on another and thus help evolve a greater sense of our true worth and needs.

Medicinal properties: Lady's mantle is primarily used to regulate menstrual bleeding. It can be used both internally and externally such as in a douche for treating leucorrhea (vaginal discharge). It can also be used for treating diarrhea.

Dose/Preparation: The herbal essence may be taken in one- to four-drop doses as needed to foster self-acceptance and courage in intimate communication with another. Carry a small pouch of dried herb as a talisman to foster the power of self-acceptance in one-to-one communications with others.

Medicinally, the herb can be given in a standard infusion using up to one ounce of the leaves steeped in a pint of boiling water for ten to twenty minutes. Two or three cups may be taken per day. Take ten to thirty drops of the tincture three times each day.

THIS HERB SHOULD BE AVOIDED DURING PREGNANCY.

Key words: Clarity and knowledge of needs and desires of the self or others. Self-acceptance. Appreciation of one's limitations and gifts. Moodiness. Empathy for another or, instead, collapsing into another's problems.

Affirmation: "I receive satisfaction and joy in sharing the cup of my beingness with another."

Herbal allies: Chaste berries, raspberry leaf, black haw.

King of Cups

Saw Palmetto

King of Cups

Saw Palmetto; serrenoa
Fire of Water

A king sits upon his throne holding his chalice of love and desires. He is surrounded by the sea of the subconscious which contains his emotions, inspirations, and dreams. The fish symbolizes his ability to move in these underwater depths to indulge his visions, fantasies, or erotic reveries. Being imbued with a strong, passionate nature, he learns how to master his emotions through detached awareness. The king of cups has at his disposal the power of creative imagination, which may be channelled into his relationships or into visionary expressions in the areas of business, law, divinity, art, music, science, or the healing arts.

If the king should get clouded about the issues at hand he can be as violent as King Titan, god of the sea, who could create turmoil and horrendous waves due to his jealousy and imaginings. He may become obsessed with scandal, sex, deviousness, and the dark crafts.

Saw Palmetto

Spiritual properties: Saw palmetto symbolizes reproductive and creative energies. These energies can be squandered in sexual exploits or they can be sublimated and used to increase inner potency and creativity.

Medicinal properties: The small red berries of the saw palmetto make a nutritious tonic useful for those who are suffering from wasting and deficiency diseases. They are used for asthma, bronchitis, and colds caused by weakness and being run-down. Because it increases muscular bulk and flesh, it is particularly useful for athletes. In addition, it is used for loss of sexual power in both men and women. Combined with echinacea and damiana, it is used for treating prostate conditions.

Dose/Preparation: For spiritual purposes, the dried berries can be worn in a pouch or strung into a bracelet or necklace and worn to increase physical and emotional potency. For example, for sexual frigidity, the berries might be worn as a belt around the waist or genital areas to help open up sexual energy. For increasing heartfelt emotions, wear the berries near the heart. The essence can be taken a few times daily accompanied with an appropriate affirmation so that your inner king of cups is strengthened in a positive way.

A therapeutic dose of two capsules or ten to thirty drops of the tincture is taken three times daily. The tincture must be prepared from the fresh berries.

Key words: Intimacy and openness. Cultivating masculine sensitivity. The ability to receive as well as to give of one's self. Developing one's capacity for close sharing. Erotic potential. Need to open up creatively and/or sexually. Giving counsel or care to others. Detached observer or emotional excesses.

Affirmation: "I am open to giving and receiving in an intimate way."

Herbal allies: Dong quai for women, ginseng for men.

SUIT OF WANDS

Ace of Wands

Yarrow

Ace of Wands

Yarrow; Achillea Millefolium
Root Power of Fire

A hand emerges from the clouds embracing a wand and a sprig of yarrow. The life-force of the Spirit is fully acknowledged and accepted. The shafts of light are the inner illumination that one can experience. It is time for revelation and enlightenment. Be willing to face the truth, whatever it may be.

The card also represents triumph and success of an endeavor or project. All one needs to do to be assured of success is to learn the power of consistency in endeavor, to pace oneself accordingly, and to follow an enterprise through to completion.

Yarrow

Spiritual properties: Yarrow has the capacity to open the mind and the seventh chakra to inspirations and revelations from Spirit. It is cleansing to the body and the aura and will offer protection against invasive thought forms. One will hear one's own internal music more clearly as the blockages are cleared.

Medicinal properties: Long associated with the divinatory I Ching of the Chinese, yarrow is a common wayside herb found in diverse areas of the world. It is assigned to this ace because it promotes warmth and circulation throughout the body and throughout one's being.

The leaves and blossoms promote sweating for the treatment of fevers, colds, and flu. They aid digestion, relieve menstrual cramps, staunch bleeding, and generally assist blood circulation throughout the body. For fevers, they can be combined with elder flowers, peppermint, boneset, cayenne, and ginger. For high blood pressure, yarrow is combined with hawthorn flowers, linden flowers, and European mistletoe.

Dose/Preparation: The herb can be carried in a pouch and taken as an herbal essence to increase intuitive atunement between the inner and outer aspects of being. The umbel (flower head) can be meditated with to help one to be as open to the inspirations from heaven as this flower is.

Medicinally, the herb is taken in tea or alcoholic extract (tincture). The tea is made by steeping an ounce of the dried leaves and flowers in a pint of boiling water, covered until cool enough to drink warm. Ten to thirty drops of the extract are taken three times daily as needed.

Key words: Directness. Insights and breakthroughs. Enlightenment. Simplicity. Harmony.

Affirmation: "I am a child of the universe. I embrace the illuminations revealed."

Herbal allies: Boneset, chrysanthemum flowers, peppermint.

Two of Wands

Two of Wands

Basil; Ocimum basilicum
Mars in Aries

A noble youth holds the globe in his hand, surveying the unlimited options and possibilities it encompasses. He indicates genuine appreciation of his status and accomplishments. If this is an expanded state of awareness it can be the very essence of positiveness, but, in a lesser sense, it can border on conceit and aloofness. Here lie the ideas of mastery over one's desires and of self-control. This card teaches us to guard against the complacency and inertia that often occurs among those who are materially blessed yet spiritually empty. Lacking a spiritual perspective on material gains and wealth may create a tendency to mere dreaminess and an inability to follow through with projects one has begun.

Basil

Spiritual properties: Basil will help develop, reveal, and use the enthusiastic fire element within. It supports idealism and keeps inner vision clear. It is one of the most sacred plants of India and is said to open the heart and mind, clear the aura, and give strength to the immune system. Holy basil, sacred to both Krishna and Vishnu, is revered in the Hindu household. It protects against contagious diseases and negative influences and is burned as an incense and disinfectant.

Medicinal properties: The word basil descends from the Greek *basileus,* or king. Herbalists have long associated it with royalty and nobility. Parkinson says, "the smell thereof is so excellent that it is fit for a king's house." At the same time a quite contrary association gives it the power to attract scorpions. As a result of this, Culpepper upholds the belief that "every like draws its like," and the herb can be used as an external poultice to draw out the poisons of venomous snakes and stings.

Primarily, basil is used to stimulate perspiration for the treatment of colds, flu, and fevers as well to aid the release of inner tensions of spirit.

Dose/Preparation: Fresh basil may be worn and smelled throughout the day to invoke the powers of protection and inspiration and to help elevate self-esteem. Growing a plant in the house will keep the area cleared of negativity and will take in the positive ions and energize negative ions. The essence may be taken throughout the day to aid in acknowledging inner ideals and bringing them into manifested reality.

Medicinally, a teaspoon of the dried leaves is steeped in a covered cup of boiling water until cool enough to drink, three or four cups being taken daily. Sweet basil is widely used as a flavoring condiment, especially in Italian cuisine. The tea can be taken occasionally for gas and indigestion.

Key words: Self-confidence. Self-worth. Confidence. Following one's inspiration with action. Being protected in one's endeavors.

Affirmation: "With self-confidence and inner mastery I move forward with my choices in life."

Herbal allies: Yerba buena, oregano, marjoram, thyme.

Three of Wands

Three of Wands

Saffron; Crocus sativus
Sun in Aries

An adventurer stands on a sandy beach looking seaward. He observes a sailing vessel approaching the shore. The card represents the beginning or continuation of a venture or experience. The boat in the distance signals the potential and hopes that such a venture brings. It further symbolizes an opportunity that is waiting for recognition. The individual standing alone on the shore needs to make an effort to extend himself and to make his needs and desires known to others. Thus, the uneven number three represents instability or a cycle of going forth.

The herb saffron symbolizes the fiery element needed to move forward with one's desires and has the ability to stimulate inner warmth and digestion of experiences.

Saffron

Spiritual properties: Saffron will help to stimulate the digestion of experiences and will help in the healthful assimilation of the lessons learned. It will impart the energy of love and devotion and will help one to see one's part in the dance of life more clearly.

Medicinal properties: Saffron consists of the yellow stigmas of the crocus. Because it is so light and difficult to harvest in quantity it is one of the most valuable botanicals. It figures prominently as a culinary spice, imparting a pleasing flavor and an attractive yellowish color to a variety of foods, such as rice. It also is an aid to digestion and is useful for conditions arising from digestive weakness. It is primarily a blood vitalizer, regulates menses in women, and, in large doses, can cause miscarriage.

SAFFRON SHOULD NOT BE TAKEN DURING PREGNANCY.

Dose/Preparation: Carry a pinch of the herb in a pouch to help manifest the positive lessons of this card. Meditations with saffron or its cousin the common crocus will help to center oneself and to vitalize the third (solar plexus) and fourth (heart) chakras. Take the essence once per day in the morning to aid in digesting and assimilating the day's experiences.

Medicinally, only a small amount is used—about 100 to 500 milligrams. It can be combined with food or served in boiled warm milk with honey. Corcine is a powerful yellow pigment and makes a fine yellow dye. Even a 1 part per 100,000 solution will turn water yellow.

Key words: Possibilities. Getting on with it. Movement. Making one's needs and desires known. Recognizing the opportunities presented.

Affirmation: "This is the first day of the rest of my life. I go forth with inner strength and confidence."

Herbal allies: Safflower, calendula blossoms.

Four of Wands

Fennel Seed

Four of Wands

Fennel Seed;
Foeniculum vulgare
Venus in Aries

In many ancient traditions it is the angels, or devas, who concern themselves with the maintenance of all existence and life. Here we find two of these experiencing the joy of a day's completion. Implicit in this scene is the subtle need to release the tension and pressure involved in completing a task and to experience completion before going on to the next task. How do we do this? Making time to be together and play is one important method which also teaches the value of cooperation and prevents the dangers of egocentricity and overseriousness.

Another message of this card is to allow talents and skills to flow and be shared. Be unafraid to live up to your potential. Allow your inner light to shine through.

Fennel Seed

Spiritual properties: Fennel will allow a greater sense of groundedness and joy to permeate one's being. Rub fennel oil on the soles of the feet and dance to the rhythms of life. Crush a fresh sprig of fennel and let its smell fill you with healing earth energy and help you to release any hesitations you may have with regards to finishing the project at hand. Play with life more and find friends with whom you can share some fun.

Medicinal properties: Fennel stalks and roots are eaten as a food like celery. Taken as a tea, the seeds are commonly useful for stimulating appetite and digestion and are used to eliminate gas. The seeds are also useful to relieve a variety of abdominal pains including menstrual cramps. Having properties very similar to anise seed, fennel seed has calming effects on bronchitis and coughs and can be used to flavor cough remedies. An infusion (strong tea) of the seeds is also useful as an eyewash to treat pink eye (conjunctivitis) and inflammation of the eyelids (blepharitis) when applied externally as a warm compress. Fennel seed tea seems to be very effective in increasing the flow of nursing mother's milk. For this, it is often combined with marshmallow root which increases the richness of the milk. Dry roasted, the seeds are taken to relieve pain of the testes and urinary bladder.

Dose/Preparation: Carry fennel seeds in a pouch and smell them during the day so that you can breath in their message. Use the oil as well for this purpose. The herbal essence may be taken to reinforce the idea of playfulness.

Medicinally, for abdominal pains, indigestion, and gas, steep a teaspoon of the crushed seeds in a covered cup of boiling water. Fennel is good to take after meals and first thing in the morning to help regulate digestion and the circulation of energy through the body. It is quite useful for gynecological complaints and as an expectorant for coughs.

Key words: Completion. Pleasant thoughts. Moving on to the next cycle. Dancing and movement with life. Comradeship. Shared success.

Affirmation: "I feel greater self-confidence by quietly recognizing my many gifts and accomplishments."

Herbal allies: Anise seed, star anise, cumin seed.

Five of Wands

Turmeric; Curcuma longa
Saturn in Leo

Here we have five hands, representing differences of race and political alliance, brandishing their staffs in a contentious manner. The card represents strife, prejudice, conflict, opposition, and disagreement. Such conflict and rivalries can drain our energies and divert us from more fruitful pursuits and endeavors. Even wars are not possible when our thoughts and efforts are fruitfully preoccupied with building strength from within. Therefore, to feel threatened is to betray an inner weakness that is better examined before we react.

Let us not forget that, when open conflict seems the only choice, it represents, in some way, a personal failure in dealing with our own shortcomings as well as an inability to communicate that which we feel to be vital to our survival and well-being. It is always worth considering the innate weakness and vulnerability that has led us to such confrontations and whether strengthening those areas of weaknesses might not be of greater value. By doing so, we might have the best chance of averting further loss and decimation of reserves that is attendant to all conflicts.

Turmeric

Spiritual properties: When one feels a lack of strength and spiritual power, this herb will fortify and create an inner stirring of strength. For those whose energy is aggressive and argumentative, it will clear this energy and create the space for a new and healthier viewpoint to grow.

Medicinal properties: Turmeric root is included as an herb of the fire element because of its warm, stimulating effects on digestion and circulation together with its spicy and bitter flavor. It is an aromatic stimulant and carminative. It is a basic ingredient of "curry," or *garam masala*, an Indian spice combination that blends exotic spices such as coriander, cumin seed, asafetida, and cayenne pepper to stimulate appetite by adding flavor and color to aid the digestion and assimilation of food.

Turmeric has been used to successfully regulate blood sugar levels in some cases and helps to diminish PMS (premenstrual syndrome) symptoms and regulate menses. It is one of the most valuable herbs for the prevention and treatment of gallstones.

Dose/Preparation: Carry some turmeric in a pouch to remind you of the spiritual tenacity that is needed in life. Use the herbal essence as needed to further augment the lessons indicated by this card.

Medicinally, two capsules can be taken three to six times daily over the course of one to three months for gallstones, diabetes, menstrual irregularities, and liver dysfunction, including hepatitis. Taken with food, it aids digestion and assimilation, especially when combined with cumin and coriander seed.

Key words: Opposition. Strife. Suppression. Disagreement. Conflict. Need to look inward for the conflict that is manifested as an outward occurrence.

Affirmation: "Anger is the measure of fear. Love is the measure of faith."

Herbal allies: Barberry root, bupleurum root.

Six of Wands

Six of Wands

**Hawthorn;
Crataegus oxycanthae
Jupiter in Leo**

A warrior appears triumphant after a minor conflict. The mood is one of tentative victory. The contenders have left their staves (wands) behind and seem to have deserted the battlefield. Perhaps they have decided that the prize is not, after all, worth the struggle, thus leaving the victor the problem of confronting the true worth of his achievement.

Be sure that what you are struggling to achieve is worth the price of time and energy expended. You may find others acquiescing and stepping aside simply because they have decided the possible gain is not worth the potential loss. The exception to this is the value of undergoing a challenging or difficult task for the sake of personal growth and realization. Such exercises are often done as an initiation rite. Remember, however, each moment of our lives offers an opportunity to rise above our limitations. We may not be up to them all so we should learn to choose those opportunities that offer the most good for all.

This may be a time for self-confidence and pride in leadership and teamwork abilities. Be open for messages from within or from the world around you as to what you are to do next.

Hawthorn

Spiritual properties: The hawthorn will help to release a person from feelings of disharmony and even hate. It will reinstate inner calm and poise after a period of conflict and struggle. The heart chakra will be fortified and a greater sense of ease and self-love will be renewed.

Medicinal properties: Hawthorn berries combine mildly sedative and calming properties. Herbalists regard it as a gentle but effective remedy for problems of the heart and the circulatory system. As such, it is used for arteriosclerosis, angina pectoris, and high blood pressure. For high blood pressure, hawthorn berries are taken alone or in combination with yarrow, European mistletoe, cayenne, and linden flowers. Some herbalists believe that the flowers and leaves possess a greater concentration of the active principle than the berries. The Chinese consider the sour flavor of hawthorn berries useful to stimulate appetite and aid digestion. It is especially regarded as being an effective aid for the digestion and assimilation of dense proteins, such as meats.

Dose/Preparation: Use the herbal essence to fortify the energy of the heart and to foster feelings of self-love and love for those with whom you have been in conflict. Wear some of the berries in a pouch near the heart as a reminder of the inner place of calm that can be the basis of your being.

Medicinally, hawthorn berries make a pleasant and somewhat sour tea. Simply simmer one or two tablespoons of the crushed berries in a cup of boiling water. The tincture may be taken, a dropperful three times per day.

Hawthorn berries should not be used with ulcers, colitis, or heart conditions that display excess heat in the body. Use the herbal essence instead.

Key words: Victory. Confidence. Satisfaction. Self-confidence. Message from within as to the direction to take. Calmness of heart. Assurance.

Affirmation: "I confidently move forward in the direction that my heart dictates."

Herbal allies: Rose hips, cranberries.

Seven of Wands

Seven of Wands

Wild Ginger; Asarum canadense
Mars in Leo

The seeker in this card has the opportunity to confront his or her problems and obstacles. He is different from the figure on the five of wands in that he chooses to view his goal or objective with greater confidence and as an experience worthy of more sustained determination.

The lesson of this card is one of steadfastly holding on to what you believe and, by doing so, overcoming all obstacles. Becoming clearer as to what is truly important, you are able to summon the strength to undergo whatever is necessary to achieve your just objective. It is time to be true to yourself and your beliefs despite criticism. Take a look at how you can present your ideas so that you are effective and understood.

Wild Ginger

Spiritual properties: Presenting a perfect heart-shaped leaf, wild ginger is naturally found in the shaded areas of forests. Here it serves to remind us to not lose heart even as we pass through the densest thicket and the darkest moments of our life. It will stimulate in us the need to be brave and to face our fears with spiritual tenacity.

Medicinal properties: The rhizome of wild ginger is used to relieve blood congestion and promote blood circulation. It is classified as an emmenagogue, which helps precipitate and promote blood circulation in both men and women. Since blood stagnation is one of the primary causes of pain, wild ginger can be used to disperse swelling and cysts as well as relieving arteriosclerosis. It is very helpful when combined with hawthorn berries for valvular heart problems and for helping to clear the veins and arteries. This is especially useful for the aged. It can also be used for the first stages of colds, coughs, fevers, and flu. It is very warming and helps to sweat out illnesses.

Dose/Preparation: The dried rhizome can be worn as a talisman and the herbal essence taken as needed to guide us through dark and troubled moments. It will remind us of the inner strength and guidance that is there for us to tap into on our journey.

Medicinally, since the volatile oils of wild ginger contain the primary active principle, the herb should only be steeped, not boiled, in a covered container using up to one ounce of herb to a pint of boiling water. One cup is taken occasionally or two or three times daily for a week or two to correct acute problems. For chronic circulatory problems, it should be combined with other herbs such as dong quai, angelica, or hawthorn berries.

GINGER SHOULD NOT BE TAKEN BY PREGNANT WOMEN, AS IT IS AN EMMENAGOGUE.

Key words: Challenge. Valor. Competition. Standing up for one's beliefs. Finding inner strength.

Affirmation: "I have within me the capacity to rise to any challenge and surmount any obstacle."

Herbal allies: Cultivated ginger, cayenne.

Eight of Wands

Sassafras; Sassafras albidum
Mercury in Sagittarius

Eight of Wands

Eight staves fly swiftly toward an undefined target. The card represents the need for focused, swift, and efficient action to deal with the problems at hand. Goal in sight, we are presented with a variety of diversions and problems, perhaps as a test of our resolve to continue the quest.

The absence of a human figure on the card suggests that at such times of crises we may temporarily lose our sense of self in the various problems and concerns with which we are dealing. It may be time for quick action and clarity in communication. Be willing to express your ideas and to break through the blockages that present themselves to you. Work at establishing a greater communication between the higher, sublime self and the beings and angels that guide you, for you may find greater clarity as to what is to be done next.

Sassafras

Spiritual properties: Sassafras opens up the fifth chakra (throat) and allows easier communication of ideas. It enhances the connection you have with angelic beings that watch over you. Sassafras affords you greater psychic protection against the negative effects of external harassment and attack. It will ward off or lessen the blows of conflicting forces.

Medicinal properties: Sassafras is useful both as a circulatory stimulant and as a detoxifying blood purifier. It has warming energy and is useful to induce perspiration for the early treatment of colds, flu, and coughs. It is also an effective cleansing herb for urinary problems. All these properties combine to make it one of the most effective blood purifiers for treatment of acne as well as many other skin disorders.

One of the ingredients of sassafras, safrole, has been found to have carcinogenic tendencies (safrole is naturally found in a variety of other common herbs, such as basil.) For this reason sassafras has been banned by the United States Food and Drug Administration as a natural flavoring agent in commercial root beer. It seems, however, that the safrole in sassafras, while being capable of extraction in alcohol, does not extract in water, making it safe for use in herb tea.

Dose/Preparation: The herbal essence may be used as needed and the talisman may be worn to bring about spiritual results. It may be a good idea to meditate while taking the herb and gently ask for the guidance that you seek. Keep yourself open for whatever communication is given to you and write it down. This may help you to establish the communication needed between the sublime self and the outer manifested self. The goals will be clearer and the direction more defined.

Medicinally, sassafras has been and continues to be regarded as a common healthful folk beverage and food spice by mountain folk of the Appalachian and Ozark ranges. Further, the areas where it has been traditionally consumed have noticeably low rates of cancer. Sassafras tea is made by steeping a teaspoon to a tablespoon of the root bark in a cup of boiling water, covered for ten to twenty minutes. One cup may be taken three times daily.

Key words: Lots of ideas coming in at once. Communication needed. Rapid developments. New ideas about philosophy on life. Making fast decisions.

Affirmation: "I respond to challenges with decisive clarity and vigor."

Herbal allies: Cinnamon twigs and branches.

Nine of Wands

Bayberry Bark

Nine of Wands

**Bayberry Bark; Myrica cerifera
Moon in Sagittarius**

The warrior sits beneath the tree, staff in hand, while eight other staffs present a barrier of opposition in the not too distant horizon. Unable to vanquish his foes, he also remains unvanquished. Thus, the card signifies a formidable opposition or condition presenting itself in your life. Watchfulness is of the utmost importance as you avail yourself of the opportunity to gather your reserves and prepare for an impending confrontation.

The card also serves as a reminder that, more often than not, we are our own worst enemy. The nature of any confrontation may challenge and distract us from knowledge of self, yet the experience can help us to see the mirror of ourselves through the situation at hand. Success in dealing with such experiences, therefore, is to seek a greater knowledge of self. Strength is found when one takes the opportunity to reflect on the inner state which predisposed one to the present conflict.

This card may also represent a time of feeling most whole, balanced, and grounded. Due to the place of inner power cultivated within, there may be a feeling of great inner strength and an ability to see a conflict for what it is and not feel unduly threatened by it.

Bayberry Bark

Spiritual properties: This herb will strengthen and coalesce reserves in the face of adversity and opposition. Areas of inner conflict and self-invalidation will be made more visible, and the energy of attracting conflict toward the self will be lessened.

Medicinal properties: Bayberry bark combines both warm, stimulating, and drying astringent properties. It is used to inhibit or slow all abnormal discharges including abnormal mucus discharge from the sinuses and lungs, diarrhea, bleeding, and excessive menstrual bleeding. It is also used for the treatment of colds and coughs, especially when there is an excess of clear or whitish phlegm. Finally it makes an excellent tooth and gum powder for whitening and tightening the teeth and treating gingivitis or gum inflammation.

Dose/Preparation: Use the herbal essence as needed and visualize the self being strong and whole. See the area of inner conflict and turmoil melting away and allow a clear blue light to fill their space. Carry the herb in a pouch to imbue you with the cohesiveness that is needed.

Key words: Fortification. Holding off. Suspicion. Feeling of wholeness.

Affirmation: "I feel inner balance and groundedness. I face any opposition with peace and understanding."

Herbal allies: Oak bark, witch hazel.

Ten of Wands

Prickly Ash Bark;
Zanthoxylum americanum
Saturn in Sagittarius

The full bundle of ten wands are carried as a burden on the back of the voyager. The sense is of being overwhelmed, oppressed, and weighted down by various cares and concerns. While there is less opportunity for distractions and diversions, there is an obvious opportunity for organizing and gaining clearer focus and vision. Adhering to priorities can generate focused energy that will bring the reward of important personal breakthroughs.

Take the opportunity to become organized in all aspects of your being. Clarify your goals. Make sure you allow others to take on their responsibilities as well. There is no need for you to take on other people's loads. A lot can be accomplished when this energy is handled properly.

Prickly Ash Bark

Spiritual properties: The herb will relieve feelings of oppression and burden. The idea that one is a martyr and victim will slowly be transformed to seeing the self as a creator and a responsible being. There is no need for or virtue in chewing and digesting someone else's experiences and lessons. It will be seen that it is better to allow others to face their own karma and responsibility while you remain in detached compassion.

Medicinal properties: The inner bark of prickly ash combines both stimulating and detoxifying properties. It is used to treat various circulatory disorders, including arthritic and rheumatic problems, coldness, and abdominal pains. It is also used as an alterative, with other detoxifying herbs such as chaparral, red clover blossoms, stillingia, and dandelion, for treating cancer. By strongly promoting circulation it relieves various congestive pains including those described above, cold stomach pains (gastralgia), pain from traumas and injuries, as well as pain from cysts and lumps caused by congestion or stagnation of fluids and blood.

Dose/Preparation: The herbal essence is taken and the talisman of dried herbs is worn to relieve negative feelings of oppression and burden.

Medicinally, simmer an ounce of the root bark in a covered pint of boiling water for ten to twenty minutes. One cup should be taken two or three times daily.

Key words: Oppression. Heaviness. Breakthroughs. Taking responsibility for one's own karma and creations. Allowing others to take on their own loads of responsibilities. Seeing one's goals and doing the work necessary to achieve them.

Affirmation: "I willingly take on my responsibilities and allow others to take on theirs as well."

Herbal allies: Chaparral, dandelion.

Page of Wands

Shepherd's-purse

Page of Wands

**Shepherd's-purse;
Capsella bursa-pastoris
Earth of Fire**

The page of wands depicts a youthful traveler looking at a sunrise. The card symbolizes the dawning of new opportunities. There is still a way to travel to achieve one's final goal and there is the assurance of its presence in the not too distant future.

The page symbolizes a youth who is looking for the best place to use his boundless enthusiasm and energy. Such an individual may need to come to the realization that his innate fear and insecurity is preventing a deepening of experience. Because of this, there is a tendency to hold himself back from the rewards and satisfaction of forming deep and lasting commitments.

Shepherd's-purse

Spiritual properties: Shepherd's-purse invigorates the life-force within and helps one to recognize and implement talents and abilities that have been hidden. It strengthens the will and spiritual tenacity.

Medicinal properties: Shepherd's-purse is primarily used as an astringent to stop bleeding. It is especially useful for excessive vaginal and urinary bleeding. There is the sense of regulating fire by regulating bleeding. Shepherd's-purse is also known as a blood purifier (alterative) and eliminates excess water from the body (diuretic).

Dose/Preparation: A talisman can be worn of the seeds to inspire hope and opportunity. The herbal essence is taken frequently throughout the day for the same purpose. Visualize yourself looking out to the sunrise and walking your path with inner strength and courage.

For medicinal uses if there is excessive bleeding, it is best to use the tincture of the fresh herb; thirty drops three times per day. Use it alone or with other complementary herbs in formulas for excessive menstrual bleeding, genitourinary problems, difficult urination, and postpartum bleeding. A standard infusion is one ounce of the dried herb or two ounces of the fresh, steeped in a pint of boiling water, covered until cool enough to drink. Take one cup three or more times daily.

Key words: Optimism. New dawn. Hope. Opportunity. Acknowledging inner strength and talents.

Affirmation: "With all fears and insecurities aside, clarity and single mindedness is the key to my success."

Herbal allies: Uva ursi, manzanita.

Knight of Wands

Knight of Wands

Aconite; Aconitum napellus
WARNING: POISON!
Air of Fire

The knight of wands represents the expanding and volatilizing aspect of fire. He is an armored, hot-blooded warrior ready to take on a cause vigorously. If a woman draws the card, the knight of wands would be most like the character Brünnhilde in Wagner's Ring Cycle, an enthusiastic female warrior whose exuberant personality tends to align with and champion various causes.

The knight of wands is bold and unafraid to act quickly and with great courage. He must guard against becoming too "macho" and insensitive. Such an individual does best when he directs his competitive spirit to overcoming personal shortcomings and limitations rather than trying to dominate and control others who are of a more yielding nature. If he is at all intelligent, he will learn for himself the power or simplicity of yielding. It would be better for his life expression, however, if he could learn this sooner rather than later for then he could direct his boundless energy and will to personal spiritual growth and service to others.

Aconite

Spiritual properties: The herb may be carried as a talisman to maximize potential and overcome indifference and apathy. It will stimulate the fire within and help one to move out of fixed conditions.

Medicinal properties: ACONITE, ALSO KNOWN AS MONKSHOOD, IS ONE OF THE DEADLIEST PLANT POISONS KNOWN. It is taken either in a minute homeopathic dose or in a specially prepared and detoxified form (Aconitum praeparatum) called *fu zi* that is used in traditional Chinese medicine. It is the most yang herb and the most powerful metabolic stimulant known. It is used for coldness, low metabolism, and arthritic and rheumatic complaints. Usually it is combined with other complementary herbs such as ginger, cinnamon, atractylodes, and licorice root.

Dose/Preparation: A talisman of the herb may be worn or a meditation may be practiced with the herb or with the card. Envision the warming stimulating energy flowing through you and allow the exuberant energy to fill you. Use this energy to overcome personal blockages and limitations.

For medicinal use, take homeopathically in the third to thirtieth potency (see glossary: Homeopathy and Homeopathic potency) for all conditions caused by a shock to the system. When taken frequently, every half hour from one to six doses, it is often very effective in preventing a cold or flu from developing. It seems to rally the body's defenses against external pathogenic factors. It is also good to take after an emotional shock to prevent a more chronic sickness from developing.

Prepared aconite is made by neutralizing the deadly poisonous alkaloids through a traditional process evolved by the Chinese. In this form it is quite harmless for those individuals who might benefit from its use. It is usually in special combinations. One should, however, not take more than one half to one gram once or twice a day. It is contraindicated for individuals who complain of excessive heat and/or constipation.

A homeopathic essence of the *prepared* root is similarly taken, no more than one drop daily.

Key words: Determination. Dominance. Conquest. Zeal. Willful intention. Crusader.

Affirmation: "However it may manifest, I have universal power at my command and I can and do make a difference."

Herbal allies: Cayenne or black pepper, ginger, cloves, galangal.

Queen of Wands

Queen of Wands

Raspberry Leaf; Rubus idaeus
Water of Fire

The queen of wands represents the watery/yin aspect of fire. She is depicted as a Native American whose earthiness is symbolized by her fertility. She is a woman in full possession of her feminine powers and radiates an aura of profound inner calm and groundedness.

The queen may have a tendency to allow herself to become inundated and overwhelmed with practical matters. She can find deeper satisfaction and rewards if she remembers to cultivate and maintain her innate feminine intuitive powers. She may also need to make more time for shared intimacy and for allowing the inner child to emerge in a playful way.

157

Raspberry Leaf

Spiritual properties: Raspberry leaf helps one tune into the child within and allows natural enthusiasm for life to be manifested. It will soften the heart and allow for greater receptivity and intuition.

Medicinal properties: The raspberry has many uses that are considered beneficial to women. The fruit is used as a blood tonic and helps nourish the female reproductive system. The leaves are traditionally used to regulate menses and to prepare the womb for childbirth. In Western herbalism, raspberry leaf tea is universally used, either alone or in combination with other herbs, in formulas for women. Further, having a cool energy, it can also be generally used by all for the treatment of simple acute conditions such as colds and flu. Its astringent property makes it useful internally to treat diarrhea and bleeding and externally as a poultice for cuts, wounds, and abrasions.

Dose/Preparation: The talisman may be worn or the herbal essence of raspberry leaf may be taken three times per day to promote fertility and receptivity. Visualize the child within emerging in a joyous way with enthusiasm and creativity.

Medicinally, this herb is useful to take throughout pregnancy, one or two cups per day. It softens and makes the womb more pliable for easier delivery. It also will help to prevent miscarriage and lessen postpartum bleeding. It can be made as a beverage tea, one teaspoon per cup of boiling water, or it may be made as an infusion for stronger medicinal purposes.

Key words: Sensuality. Feminine warmth. Inner poise and command. Potency. Getting in touch with the child within.

Affirmation: "Discretion and receptivity are the keys to my power."

Herbal allies: Blackberry leaf, thimbleberry leaf.

King of Wands

Cinnamon

King of Wands

Cinnamon;
Cinnamomum zeylanicum
Fire of Fire

The king of wands represents the fiery aspect of fire. This is symbolized by the deep red shirt and desert landscape. The blue outer cape suggests the power and capacity to contain heat. Thus, there is great reserve of inner strength.

The king enjoys the feeling of power and control and has the capacity and energy to use it whenever required. He must learn that there may be virtue in holding back this energy in certain situations and he must guard against any tendency towards over-reaction, impulsiveness, or cruelty.

For those who have a lack of the positive aspect of the fire power, it may be time to start developing and finding the inner motivation and decisiveness that the fiery king represents.

Cinnamon

Spiritual properties: Cinnamon helps build the internal fire and will. Its warm energy can dissipate inner coldness and allow the creative fires to burn.

Medicinal properties: Cinnamon bark combines both sweet and spicy flavors that deeply stimulate metabolism and circulation. It is classified as a warming stimulant, tonic, diuretic (gets rid of excess water), carminative (relieves gas), astringent (constricting and binding effect), and analgesic (relieves pain). It is useful for all diseases caused by coldness including cold extremities, weak digestion with abdominal cramps and spasms, and common colds.

Dose/Preparation: A talisman of the dried bark can be worn to generate greater motivation and warmth. The essence is taken internally to help increase drive and focus.

For medicinal uses, cinnamon bark can be used for diarrhea and most fevers by steeping a teaspoon of powered herb in a cup of boiling water, with three cups taken daily. For coldness, weak digestion, and the first stages of the common cold, combine with three or four slices of ginger root and a teaspoon of honey or other sweetener. Taken warm, this tea will promote sweating; cool, it will increase urination. Cinnamon boiled in milk is an effective treatment for diarrhea.

Key words: Inner strength and fire. Competition. Impulsiveness. Decisiveness. Fire used in fierce and cruel way. Need to warm up inside. Motivation.

Affirmation: "I acknowledge my inner fires and use my strength to direct my destiny."

Herbal allies: Black pepper, pippli pepper, cloves, ginger.

THE SUIT OF SWORDS

Ace of Swords

Ace of Swords

Chamomile; Anthemis nobilis
Root Power of Air

An angelic hand piercing the clouds grasps the hilt of a double-edged sword which supports a celestial crown. This card symbolizes the expansion of thoughts, enlightenment, and illumination. There is a need to have clarity of mind and to affirm inner truths.

As with all two-edged swords, there is another side. One must watch that actions, determination, and strength do not turn into excessive use of force, excessive thinking, or extremes in desires, otherwise the end result will be weakness, instability, nervous energy, and self-destruction. With the ace of swords, one should strive to allow creative and inspired ideas to burst forth.

The potential for peaceful resolution, unbiased thoughts, and clarity of mind are now in the forefront. This is a time when complete self-acceptance and acceptance of others are possible. Through meditation and conscious living, inner peace and contentment can be attained.

Chamomile

Spiritual properties: Chamomile bestows greater inner peace and finer clarity about one's inner spiritual purpose. There will be a more relaxed energy about seeing and working with the energies of Divine Spirit. Chamomile has the ability to enhance visions and to bring them into form on the earth.

Medicinal properties: Chamomile is one of the most widely used beverage and medicinal teas. It is a valuable calming drink for restlessness, nervous stomach, and insomnia. It is safely used for children in the treatment of colds, indigestion, and nervous disorders. Chamomile will help relieve cramping associated with the menstrual cycle and will bring on menstruation. It is high in calcium and, when allowed to grow wild, it supplies the earth with this building nutrient.

Dose/Preparation: The herbal essence may be taken throughout the day as needed. Smelling the flowers as in aroma therapy will impart the peaceful energy of this plant. The energy of chamomile helps to open the heart chakra and the third eye (sixth chakra), thus bringing greater peace and clarity to the thoughts as they will be guided by the heart's wisdom.

A beverage tea is made by steeping a tablespoon of chamomile in a pint of boiled water for ten minutes. For a stronger effect, use one half ounce of the flowers to a pint of water and drink one half cup of the tea as needed. A tincture is also used, taken one dropperful at a time.

Use chamomile with care during pregnancy, as it is a uterine stimulant.

Key words: Clarity of mind. Expansion of thoughts. Assessing the situation and making decisions. Upholding inner truths. Need to think in a more positive way.

Affirmation: "I use the clarity of my thoughts to bring me peace and illumination."

Herbal allies: Lavender, spearmint.

Two of Swords

Passionflower

Two of Swords

Passionflower;
Passiflora incarnatae
Moon in Libra

A woman stands before the ocean. Her arms cross her heart and her hands hold two swords. The moon in the background is waxing; a new cycle is beginning. The woman has come to the point of integrating the duality of the mind, that is, analysis and intuition. She has also been working on an equilibrium between the heart, the emotions, and the intellect. This process will bring tranquility and greater internal balance. Any conflict that she was having is finding a resolution. Decisions and agreements have been or can now be reached. A sense of healing wisdom is hers to manifest.

She must guard against being indecisive to the point of no action and she must learn to complete those actions and cycles she has begun. If she feels tension and confusion because of her indecisiveness, she must take time out to listen to her heart's wisdom and the uncertainties will begin to fade away.

Passionflower

Spiritual properties: Passionflower was so named by Jesuit missionaries in Peru because it was thought that its distinctive corona and petals resembled the crown of thorns that Jesus wore. The herb was said to pacify the spirit. As an herbal essence it will impart a sense of peaceful balance and tranquility. Meditations with the flower can be quite mesmerizing, similar to looking at a mandala. It brings focus and accord to the mind and heart.

Medicinal properties: Passionflower is a nervine, sedative, and antispasmodic. It treats sleeplessness, chronic insomnia, seizures, epilepsy, anxiety, and nervous tension. The fruit is rich in flavonoids and is diuretic and a nutritive tonic.

Dose/Preparation: Four or more drops of the herbal essence may be taken as needed throughout the day. Visualize yourself in the two of swords setting with the passionflower embracing you. Allow the serenity and peacefulness to fill you.

For medicinal use, a standard infusion may be made and one cup taken three times per day or a tincture may be used, ten to thirty drops per dose. Two "00" capsules may be taken three times per day.

Key words: Need to create a quietness within. Work to resolve any indecisiveness. Need to balance heart and mind. Resolving conflict. Reconciliation.

Affirmation: "Through my heart's path, I create a balance within."

Herbal allies: Zizyphus, lily of the valley.

Three of Swords

Three of Swords

Pleurisy Root;
Asclepias tuberosa
Saturn in Libra

Three swords pierce the heart, which is surrounded by dark clouds. There is a need to heal past relationships and shattered ideals. Sadness, depression, and memories of difficult separations are in one's thoughts and need to be released.

The seeds falling from the plant and the parting of the clouds convey the possibility that, since the pain is now being dealt with, one will be able to create a vision for a new beginning. A better balance will soon be reached.

Learning how to relate to others without losing oneself is important. This may be a time to become more objective toward the emotions. On the other hand, one must be careful not to use the mind to sort out the emotions, ending up in constant self-analysis and introspection. There is a need for *balance* between the emotions and the mind. This can best be accomplished through the use of herbs, meditation, and affirmations. Counselors and good listeners that work with people who are emotionally distraught with heartbreaks and trauma must learn to be more detached or their sympathies may get them embroiled with others' feelings, making their counsel less effective.

Pleurisy Root

Spiritual properties: Many times grief and sadness becomes stuck in the lungs and manifests as congestion and phlegm. An herbal essence of pleurisy root may help to relieve old emotions that need digesting and clearing out. Deep breathing and fresh air will also help.

Medicinal properties: Pleurisy root is an expectorant, diaphoretic (causes sweating), diuretic (eliminates water), and carminative. It has been used for coughs, wheezing, flu, colds, pleurisy, and other lung problems. It relieves gastritis due to slow digestion.

Dose/Preparation: The herbal essence may be taken three or four drops at a time as often as needed. Wearing a piece of pleurisy root near the heart chakra will help give relief from the feelings of emptiness and sadness associated with breakups or emotional losses.

Medicinally, a standard infusion may be made from the *dried* root. If it is drunk hot at the onset of a cold or flu it will promote sweating. Many times, colds and congestion are our body's ways of manifesting feelings of loss and grief. By sweating sickness out, we may feel better emotionally as well. The tincture may be taken in doses of five to ten drops every three hours.

Key words: Freeing oneself from past pains and heartbreaks. Working to help others find release from the past. Need to create some space for healing to occur. Becoming more of a witness to the situation.

Affirmation: "I allow the emotional pain to leave me. My heart is one with the Divine."

Herbal allies: Grindelia, white horehound.

Four of Swords

Mullein

Four of Swords

Mullein; Verbascum thapsus
Jupiter in Libra

After much disharmony, excessive thinking, and restlessness, the man has set down his sword and is taking a breather. It is time to be calm, to rest and recuperate in order to regain inner strength, reorganize thoughts, and make new plans.

This may be a good time to seek guidance spiritually, financially, or otherwise. This is not a time to be scattered and disorganized but instead one must strive to be grounded and to understand the boundaries and forms by which one must live. If there is a feeling of being repressed or restricted it is best to look to the inner realities by which one lives to see where the self is not allowed freedom of positive expression.

Any "unconsciousness" may be due to lack of the ability to confront the current situation. Take the time out to regroup and rest but do it in such a way that you will have greater strength and clarity to deal with the next step.

Mullein

Spiritual properties: Spiritually, mullein can help one to take a "breather" after much struggle and conflict. It will open the lungs and allow the life breath to flow in more easily, and allow toxins such as negative thoughts to be exhaled and released. It was worn in the past to invoke protection and it was said that if a plant was grown in the garden it would protect it as well. The soft fuzzy leaves are very soothing to the touch and can be carried in the pocket to remind the aspirant to be calm and restful.

Medicinal properties: Medicinally, mullein has been used for coughs, hoarseness, bronchitis, phlegm, and whooping cough. The flowers are specifically sedative and anti-inflammatory. The leaves are smoked alone, or with coltsfoot and yerba santa, to soothe the throat and as a substitute for tobacco.

Dose/Preparation: Taking the herbal essence will set up the internal vibration for helping one to relax and take in a healing breath. The plant may be worn as an amulet to remind one that it is time not to struggle but to recuperate and reorganize.

For all congested lung conditions, a standard infusion of mullein may be made and one cup taken three times per day, or ten to thirty drops of tincture may be taken per dose.

Key words: Need to retreat and regroup. Rest. Create more clarity and form. Get advice and information.

Affirmation: "I give myself the time to rest and recuperate, and I am open to the guidance that comes toward me."

Herbal allies: Borage, chickweed, Irish moss.

Five of Swords

Five of Swords

Mistletoe; Viscum album
Venus in Aquarius

After using unfair and devious methods a man has achieved an empty victory. He carries three swords, while two swords remain on the ground in the form of a sacrificial cross. The two people near the water feel defeated, rejected, and despondent. They see the sun in the distance being taken over by darkness rather than seeing it as a glimmer of hope and optimism.

One can be the oppressed or the oppressor. Looking at a situation as a failure is not acknowledging the lessons that are being learned and is nurturing a defeatist attitude. Likewise, looking at a situation as a conquest will set up the energy of unhealthy competition and eventual defeat. Either way is a no-win situation. The energy that sets up this situation must be released and a new attitude must be adopted. An affirmation that promotes loving allowance for the self and others is necessary. Be grateful for the lessons learned and try not to get into a win/lose way of thinking. This can truly be a turning point in one's life when one can either be honest with oneself or go into deeper deception.

Mistletoe

Spiritual properties: Mistletoe was highly revered by the Druids who ceremoniously gathered the plant from oak trees.

It was said that the mistletoe protected the wearer from all evil and that the oaks it grew upon were to be respected as well. Branches of mistletoe were carried at the ceremonies that announced the new year, which probably accounts for why it is now used during the Christmas holidays.

Another legend says that an ancient god of peace was killed by an arrow of mistletoe. His passing was deeply mourned and it was requested that he be brought back to life. He was returned to life and henceforth the mistletoe was kept safe by the goddess of love. It was asked that all those who passed under it should kiss so that it is forever remembered as a symbol of love and not hate.

Mistletoe will help develop the ability to be an "observer" to oneself and one's situations, what is known as a witness consciousness. This will allow for a greater degree of objectivity and clarity. Knotted and congested emotional or mental situations will be loosened up so that one can see things more clearly.

Medicinal properties: Mistletoe has been employed as a nervine and an antispasmodic. It calms the nervous system and treats convulsive nervous disorders, such as epilepsy. The European variety is best to use, as the North American variety has contrary properties. THE BERRIES OF ALL MISTLETOE ARE EXTREMELY TOXIC.

Dose/Preparation: Mistletoe can be worn or carried in a pouch to remind the wearer of the calmness of heart that s/he must try to embrace during the lessons of the five of swords. An herbal essence may be taken orally four or more drops at a time as needed to help plant the seeds for a new, healthier attitude. Decorate the home with a sprig of mistletoe as a reminder that love is the path. Medicinally, five drops of the tincture may be mixed in warm water to help calm the nerves and to treat spasms.

Key words: A no-win situation. Being in competition with another. Letting go of the need to be right.

Affirmation: "I let go of my judgments and allow love to be my guide."

Herbal allies: Hops, lobelia.

Six of Swords

Vervain; Verbena officinalis
Mercury in Aquarius

Six swords are traveling on a boat to a far-off shore. The sun, which can be looked at as rising or setting, indicates a new cycle beginning or an old cycle ending. The journey into a different way of viewing things has begun. A new perspective is unfolding.

Allowing the old views to leave will expose a fresh approach. Be willing to let go of the cobwebs in the mind. A new location or job or a journey may be necessary to throw one into the new perspective more completely.

However, just the willingness to allow thoughts to be open to change may be sufficient. Try to step back from your problems and situations so that a clearer perspective may be obtained.

Vervain

Spiritual properties: The history of vervain is quite fascinating. Priests called it *herba sacra* because it was used for sacrifices. The Celts used it in their anointing waters for purification during rites and rituals. Magicians and sorcerers employed an ointment of vervain. Many wore the bruised plant around the neck to prevent headaches, to help with sight, and to protect against venomous bites. It was stated that the plant opens the inner eye to other dimensions of reality.

In modern times vervain may again find a place in our seeking to see things from a different perspective by opening up the sixth chakra or third eye. It will aid in releasing "congested thinking," thus revealing new possibilities. A calmer, clearer mind is always welcomed when new energies and situations are emerging.

Medicinal properties: Vervain is an excellent herb to induce sweating and thus relieve fevers and coughs. It helps unblock constrained energy in the liver and dredges the kidneys. It is used for delayed menstrual cycles, nervousness, urinary problems, hepatitis, jaundice, insufficient mother's milk, liver congestion, and mastitis. VERVAIN IS CONTRAINDICATED DURING PREGNANCY DUE TO ITS BEING A UTERINE STIMULANT.

Dose/Preparation: A few drops of the herbal essence can be taken as often as needed when one is faced with the need to look at things from a different perspective or to see things from a different dimension of reality. A piece of the herb may be worn as a charm or amulet.

Medicinally, a standard infusion or tincture may be taken up to three times per day or used as an ointment, poultice, or wash applied to acute painful conditions such as wounds, bruises, and sprains.

Key words: Traveling in mind or body. New shores approaching. New opportunities coming your way. Fear of change. Need to relax during the ride.

Affirmation: "I open myself to different perspectives about my life; I ride in the boat of inner faith."

Herbal allies: Bupleurum, feverfew.

Seven of Swords

Seven of Swords

Wood Betony;
Betonica officinalis
Moon in Aquarius

Five swords flying through the air indicate thoughts that are ungrounded, elusive, and changeable. Only some of the information is at hand, thus two swords are in the ground. No person is visible, which indicates that confrontations are being avoided or that there are hidden intentions. There can be a sense that things are too changeable and confusing to bother about.

It may be a good time to do some research or to collect knowledge and ideas from others with regards to the scene at hand. Lay your cards on the table and be honest with yourself and with others. Be willing to reveal your true intentions or to find out and listen to what others' true intentions are. Situations like this can wear on the nerves until it is clear as to what is going on.

Wood Betony

Spiritual properties: This plant has a colorful past and has been said to have the virtue of protecting against evil spirits. It was planted in churchyards and worn as an amulet or charm to protect from "fearful visions" and drive away "devils and despair."

Betony can be employed in this fashion again to ease the mental anguish and "fearful visions" one might have when dealing with a seven of swords situation internally or externally.

Medicinal properties: Medicinally, wood betony is used as a nervine with special action for diseases of the head. Taken daily with boiled warm milk, it is a good remedy for chronic headaches. It relieves anxiety, hysteria, nervousness, and insomnia, and is often combined with other nervine herbs.

Dose/Preparation: Three or four drops of the herbal essence may be taken orally as needed. It will help clear and calm the mind and thus enable one to research and put into order the information about the situation at hand. Wearing it as an amulet or charm will help to protect against hidden intentions and deceptions and keep one from falling into playing those games as well.

Medicinally, a standard infusion can be made of wood betony and one cup taken three times per day, or ten drops of the tincture may be taken three times per day. WOOD BETONY IS CONTRAINDICATED DURING PREGNANCY DUE TO ITS BEING A UTERINE STIMULANT.

Key words: Not all things are being revealed. Need to be honest with the self and others. Research needed in order to find out what is going on.

Affirmation: "With a peaceful heart, I gather information and truth for my plans and goals."

Herbal allies: Passionflower, skullcap.

Eight of Swords

Black Cohosh

Eight of Swords

**Black Cohosh;
Cimicifuga racemosa
Jupiter in Gemini**

A bound and blindfolded man sits among swords. He is frustrated, isolated, cramped, and locked in. Situations in his life may be creating interference and blockages and may need to be looked at, but it is time not only to look at the external situation but to see how he has created the mental concepts that bind him. Are there too many ideas and thoughts coming in with no clear focus as to how to use them? Is this a time for not acting at all but instead waiting with patience and calmness until the situation changes and new circumstances arise?

Since doors are not opening maybe it is a time to rethink the direction that has been taken. It's important in situations like this to be totally in the moment and involved with present concerns. Calmness and inner quietude are in the forefront.

Black Cohosh

Spiritual properties: Black cohosh will help to relieve the cramped feeling one may have when in the midst of an eight of swords situation. There is a need to relax, be calm, and stay present without fighting the circumstances. A calmer state of mind will enhance the faculties and make a resolution easier to perceive.

Medicinal properties: Medicinally, black cohosh is a useful antispasmodic for all nervous conditions, cramps, and pains. Native Americans used black cohosh to relieve the pains associated with childbirth and with the menstrual cycle. Black cohosh has also been used for eruptive diseases, such as measles, and for rheumatism.

Dose/Preparation: Three or four drops of the herbal essence may be taken orally as often as needed. An affirmation that will induce calmness and reduce frustration will enhance the positive lessons of this card.

For medicinal use, the average dosage is one "00" capsule or five to ten drops of the tincture taken three to six times a day. Too large a dose will cause nausea and dizziness. BLACK COHOSH IS CONTRAINDICATED DURING PREGNANCY.

Key words: Need to be calm and quiet. Relooking at an issue. Feeling trapped and bound. Releasing spasms and anxieties. Releasing self-imposed limitations.

Affirmation: "By releasing myself of the thoughts that bind me, I am open to the new concepts coming my way."

Herbal allies: Blue cohosh, black haw.

Nine of Swords

Valerian

Nine of Swords

Valerian; Valeriana officinalis
Mars in Gemini

A woman sits with her hands over her face. Her gray robe is indicative of her mood. She feels guilty and judges herself too harshly. She is not looking at what is good and admirable in herself but instead she has created in her mind the idea that she is not good enough, or kind enough, or just plain "isn't enough."

Even if mistakes have been made, acknowledge them and be grateful for the lessons. The ability to look inward and examine the self is a virtuous characteristic. It may be necessary to use this tool now and make some new resolutions. This should not be done in a judgmental way that throws one into deep lamentation, grief, and shame.

Acknowledge the accomplishments in your life. Do not be afraid to see the good in your heart and deeds. All too infrequently do we truly let go of self-judgments, for self-judgment is an indication of an unhealthy ego that is afraid to view the true self and its splendor.

Valerian

Spiritual properties: Valerian will help to relieve self-judgment and the mental "spasm" in which one may indulge during trying times. When one is taking the herb or herbal essence it is helpful to say an affirmation that will reinforce the sense of one's basic goodness and worth. It may be used for self-purification when one is feeling the "guilties." It will help one to "feel warmer" toward the self.

Medicinal properties: Valerian is an antispasmodic, sedating and calming herb. It is used for all emotional disturbances and pain. However, it is not recommended for people who have a heated condition as this herb is warming and will exacerbate the condition. Valerian is best used by individuals who tend to be cooler constitutionally and have a nervous or depressed condition.

Dose/Preparation: An herbal essence may be taken as needed until the thoughts, guilt, and shame have lightened up. While taking the herb, it is best to say a positive affirmation that will reaffirm a more positive self-image.

Medicinally, a tincture made from the fresh root can be taken three or more times per day, ten to thirty drops each time. A tea made with chamomile, spearmint, and valerian can be quite soothing. Take one teaspoon of this mixture and let it steep for five minutes. Drink one or two cups per day.

Key words: Warming up to the self. Moving from self-judgment to self-acceptance. Shame and regret. Need to acknowledge one's basic goodness.

Affirmation: "I fully acknowledge my goodness and worth, for I am a child of Divine Spirit."

Herbal allies: Pennyroyal, mugwort, calamus.

Ten of Swords

Ten of Swords

Ephedra; Ephedra sinica
Sun in Gemini

The ice and snow are pierced by ten swords dripping with blood. From too much thinking and worrying, a feeling of paralysis and emptiness has arisen. One is not sure how to respond to an aspect of life. These thoughts and feelings can create the very thing that is most resisted.

Even when things look bleak and there is sadness, darkness, and depression, it is a time to embrace faith and trust and to know that this is the end of an old cycle and a new cycle will soon begin. It's time to accept things as they are; through this acceptance the light at the end of the tunnel will be seen. Using visualization, create new horizons for yourself. See yourself rising up and walking a new path with sure steps and a peaceful heart. If there is a lot of criticism, misunderstandings, and disappointments, try to remain as focused as possible and to see what opportunities are opening for you. Patience is a must.

Ephedra

Spiritual properties: An herbal essence of ephedra can be safely employed to help increase the body's ability to take in the breath thus allowing one to take in greater life-force. Just as the wind clears the air and sweeps away the old, this cleansing and clearing breath will also help to clear the mind and make way for fresh thoughts.

Medicinal properties: Ephedra, also known as ma huang, is useful for asthma, bronchitis, and other congestive conditions. It is a strong stimulant and should be used only by those who generally have a strong constitution. If it is used by those who are exhausted and have low energy it will debilitate the adrenals and create further exhaustion. Because it increases blood pressure, EPHEDRA SHOULD NOT BE USED BY THOSE WHO HAVE HYPERTENSION. IT IS CONTRAINDICATED DURING PREGNANCY.

Dose/Preparation: As an herbal essence a few drops can be taken three times a day. Get out into the natural world and feel how the trees and plants have so much wisdom and patience. They understand the forces that are around them and work with them. Allow the natural healers, the plants, to take in your dark gloom and depression. They will send it to the Mother who will transform it into rich fertilizer. Deep breathing and meditations will help to revitalize one who has been sad and in pain. Our lives have seasons and it may be time to look inward during this period and to work at rebuilding a healthy new foundation.

Medicinally, ephedra may be taken in small doses, one or two capsules a day, or in combination with other herbs that help to relieve congestion in the lungs such as goldenseal, wild cherry bark, mullein, and osha root.

Key words: Death of an old cycle. Feeling barren. Need to breathe in life more deeply. Have faith in the wisdom of the universe.

Affirmation: "I inhale and feel the cleansing energy filling me. I exhale and release the old."

Herbal allies: Cloves, eucalyptus, camphor.

Page of Swords

Page of Swords

Dill; Anethum graveolens
Earth of Air

The young page is ready to make a new start with fresh ideas and thoughts. He will sweep away all the encumbrances such as depression and negative thoughts and will make himself ready for change and new possibilities. He is like a breath of fresh air that blows away the clouds that have obscured thinking. He is your own inner child ready to learn something new. He is a freethinker and is ready to make inroads to a new reality for himself.

The page must watch that he doesn't dissipate his energy on erratic, compulsive thinking which can turn into thoughtlessness and spiteful behavior. He must not become so opinionated or fixed with his ideals that he blows everyone else away with arguments and debates.

Dill

Spiritual properties: Dill has the capacity to bring focus to attention and thoughts. It enables the user to bring out and show to the world her/his inner reality and spiritual aspirations. It will calm the air element and help one to digest new thoughts coming through.

Medicinal properties: Dill is used to treat colic, gas, indigestion, and insomnia due to indigestion. It promotes the flow of breast milk and is used to treat infant's colic.

Dose/Preparation: Dill may be taken as an essence to augment the clarity and enthusiasm of the page's energy. A piece of the herb may be carried and the aroma from the crushed seeds or leaves inhaled to bring about mental vitality and clearer focus. The air element within will be refreshed and a greater optimism will be felt.

For medicinal purposes, an ounce of powdered seeds is placed in a pint of rice wine with some chamomile flowers. This is allowed to steep for two weeks and then strained and bottled for use. Two to ten drops may be taken two or three times a day as needed. The powder may be mixed with heated honey to make a paste and this may be taken internally as needed. Chewing on a few seeds will help prevent gas and stomach "growling." A tea may be made as well, using one teaspoon of seeds to one cup of boiling water, steeped for a few minutes. If an infant has colic then the nursing mother may drink several cups of the tea and the medicinal properties will be passed to the child through the breast milk.

Key words: New thoughts. Childlike enthusiasm for innovative ideas. Pushing aside depression and negative thoughts to make a fresh start. Care in communication that it is not thoughtless and mean.

Affirmation: "I sweep away all darkness and depression and with joy I open myself to new thoughts and ideas."

Herbal allies: Peppermint, catnip, cumin, coriander.

Knight of Swords

Wild Cherry Bark

Wild Cherry Bark;
Prunus serotinae
Air of Air

The knight of swords bravely moves forward in pursuit of his ideals and dreams. An arch-defender of truth, he is willing to risk and suffer all for the sake of honesty and righteousness. He will cut through all excesses and unclarity. He is willing to speak his ideas and opinions. However, he must watch that he doesn't do this at the expense of others. Aggressive and brave in speaking his mind, he must take care that these traits do not change into willfulness, manipulation, and impatience.

Wild Cherry Bark

Spiritual properties: Wild cherry bark will enable us to relax and open up the lung energy in order to take a deeper breath, allowing ideas and thoughts to be articulated and brought out without fear and apprehension. For those who have an excess of the knight of swords energy, wild cherry bark will take the edge off any compulsiveness that may accompany "speaking one's mind."

Medicinal properties: Medicinally, wild cherry bark has been used to calm the respiratory nerves and allay coughs and asthma. It helps circulate constrained energy of the lungs, heart, and stomach. It is an outstanding remedy for weakness of the belly, such as ulcers, gastritis, colitis, and diarrhea.

Dose/Preparation: Some wild cherry bark can be placed in a pouch and worn around the lung area to remind one to take a relaxed breath before speaking in order to bring clarity to thoughts and words. Wild cherry bark essence can also be taken when one is working at perfecting the knight's energy within.

For medicinal purposes, an ounce of the herb is put into a pint of boiling water and allowed to stand covered for twenty minutes. It can also be made as a cold infusion by allowing the herbs to stand in cold water for about an hour. A sun tea can be made from wild cherry bark as well. It must not be boiled, for boiling destroys the main active constituent. One cup may be taken three times per day.

Key words: Willing to seek ideals and speak your mind. Watch for being too harsh with words. Need to consider the needs of others. Moving on to new thoughts and ideas.

Affirmation: "With strength and clarity I move forward in pursuit of my dreams and visions."

Herbal allies: Grindelia, horehound.

Queen of Swords

Lady's Slipper

Queen of Swords

Lady's Slipper;
Cypripedium pubescens
Water of Air

The queen of swords has cut through the chains of limited thinking and ideas. She stands on her own, ready to look ahead with clear vision. Her purple garment shows her openness to receiving inspirations, and her red sash indicates her willingness to manifest them. The sword in her left hand shows her unwavering intent to cut through untruth and confusion.

She stands with bare feet firmly planted on the earth, exhibiting her willingness to manifest her ideas in this reality and to remain balanced. Because of her clarity and insightfulness, she is able to help others to see themselves in a more objective and balanced way.

Her high-sightedness must not be used to be critical, vengeful, and unyielding. These ways will eventually wear on her nervous system and create tremendous imbalances to body / mind / spirit.

Lady's Slipper

Spiritual properties: This beautiful herb creates within us a deeper connection to the earth, alleviating imbalance and nervousness that can manifest when we are opening ourselves to new channels of thought. It also induces calmness and clarity when working with this type of inspiration.

Medicinal properties: Lady's Slipper relaxes the nerves, calms spasms, relieves pain and hysteria, and induces rest. It clears depression and effects a calm and cheerful state of mind. It is considered a "nerve food" and can be taken up to three times a day to help build a healthier nervous system.

Dose/Preparation: Due to its extensive use over the last century the lady's slipper is an endangered species. Like a wood nymph or spirit, it wilts and dies when taken from its natural habitant, thus it is very difficult to cultivate. When preparing lady's slipper, use it with the utmost respect and with no waste. A standard decoction can be made with it and taken two or three cups a day, or a tincture can be taken ten to thirty drops at a time.

An herbal essence would be quite effective to help induce the feelings of having your feet on the ground and your mind calm and clear, especially when doing work that entails much mental visioning and detail. Carrying lady's slipper in a pouch will transmit her magical qualities of peacefulness and joy. Meditations with the card or with a picture of the herb can have wonderful results.

Key words: Strong and independent feminine energy. Being open to inspiring ideas. Utilizing communication skills. Being too critical with words and thoughts. Seeing things from another point of view. Need to calm the mind and keep the feet on the ground. Visionary.

Affirmation: "I am willing to take my visions and dreams and share them with the world around me."

Herbal allies: Lavender flowers, calamus.

King of Swords

St. Johnswort

**St. Johnswort;
Hypericum perforatum
Fire of Air**

The king of swords sits on a rock, representing his capacity to be grounded and established in his thoughts. The sword in his left hand and his blue garment denote his innate ability to be clear in his thinking and open to innovative thoughts. The yellow garment shows his willingness to be creative and expressive with words, whether they be written or spoken. He is a natural diplomat and philosopher who can use his communication talents in ways that can be truly inspiring to others.

Through his keen ability to be analytical he is able to cut away truth from untruth. He must watch, however, that his sword is not used to be critical and harsh to himself or to those associated with him. He must be tolerant of other people's ways and not grow impatient with their slower thinking. Arrogance does not become the king of swords. He must learn to use his clarity of mind to support his creativity and to be supportive to others with whom he is associated.

St. Johnswort

Spiritual properties: This herb can impart the capacity to calm the emotions of fear, depression, and frustration in order to allow our ability for free visionary thoughts to come through. It will alleviate tension and unrest we may experience when we need to express our ideas and beliefs. For those who are stuck in arrogance about their righteousness, this herb will unstick the energy and allow a better flow to occur.

Medicinal properties: St. Johnswort is a sedative herb that strengthens and renews the nerves and raises the spirits, relieving depression. It supports the lungs, expels phlegm,and has been used to alleviate bed-wetting and internal hemorrhaging. Externally, it can be used as an ointment or compress to promote the healing of bruises, sprains, traumatic injuries, ulcers, and stings.

Dose/Preparation: As an herbal essence, the flowers and leaves may be used. It may be taken three times a day to help to incorporate the king of swords' energy. An affirmation will reinforce steadiness and calmness of mind.

Medicinally, for relief of pain due to neuralgia (spasm along a nerve), anxiety, and nervous tension, make a tea with one or two teaspoons per cup of boiling water. This may be taken two or three times daily. If a tincture is preferred, twenty drops may be taken three times per day. Externally, a liniment, poultice, or oil relieves pain and bruises. The oil is made by placing an ounce of the herb in a jar and covering it with olive oil. Let it stand in a warm place for three days and then remove the herb. Refrigerate for future use.

Key words: A seeker of truth. Apex of integrity. Arrogance with one's ideas. Being too righteous and critical. Clear communication as to what one believes. Need to remain calm and open to new ideas.

Affirmation: "I acknowledge my ability to see clearly and to communicate my beliefs and ideas."

Herbal allies: Calamus, jasmine, oatstraw.

Using the Herbal Tarot

The Herbal Tarot is not simply a tool for determining what herb should be taken for a physical problem. The rich images and symbology of the cards, and the healing modalities suggested by the herbs, offer a process through which creative free association can generate therapeutic options that may not have occurred to either querent or guide. In this way, we are able to refer to our innate authority, whether it is invoked in the name of a divinity, the subconscious mind, or simply the Higher Self.

Some who are offended by the tarot because of their religious affiliation misunderstand the meaning and intention of the cards. They are not intended to replace belief or faith in a higher divine authority, such as the Bible or Christ. The tarot is a guide for creative thought. It is like a prayer or contemplation through which divine authority can speak directly, offering inspiration for working with a problem. In this sense, a reading can begin with a prayer or invocation: "In the name of — ." Before using tarot cards, of course, one needs to make sure that the patient or client is not in any way offended by them.

The Herbal Tarot provides an excellent way to offer counseling that addresses all aspects—physical, mental, and spiritual—of a problem. It is very much in harmony with shamanistic practices as well as with neurolinguistic programming and transpersonal and Jungian psychotherapy. The concept of an herbal ally is well-known among Native American shamans who might select an herb as a guide to the herb, herbal formula, or modality that is specifically appropriate for the situation in question. Tarot cards are an excellent psycho-spiritual extension to the clinical practice of a doctor, naturopath, chiropractor, acupuncturist, or herbalist.

The great power that arises from the Herbal Tarot session is the sense that the patient-querent is generating his or her own therapeutic options. The patient, through personal involvement in choosing the cards, becomes empowered to assume full responsibility for the healing process.

All that the guide and querent need is the ability to free associate using the images and ideas suggested by the cards. One can go into a session totally open, with little or no prior knowledge of the cards. For some, in fact, this is preferred. Generally, however, the session will probably be richer if one can draw on the profound tradition of tarot symbology, which can include astrology, elemental theory, Native American teachings, kabbalism, Christian mysticism, Taoism, Sufism, or any other philosophical orientation. The more one knows about herbs, the more one can bring that physical dimension into play.

The Herbal Tarot Session

An average session using the Herbal Tarot takes about an hour to an hour and a half.

1. The querent may focus on a particular problem, whether it be mental or physical, or the reading can be on a more general topic, such as the querent's present state. While focusing on the topic of the reading, the querent looks through the deck and selects one or more cards that most symbolize the topic. These cards are placed in front of the querent.

2. The guide asks the querent to describe in his or her own terms the meaning of the cards chosen. Focus as much as pos-

sible on what is depicted on the card. The herb can be interpreted by the guide in terms of its specific properties, actions, folklore and usage, or any other aspect related to the topic of the reading. For instance, if the topic involves a health problem, such as a skin eruption or insomnia, and XV Pan is chosen, one might consider its herb, lobelia, as the herbal ally and comment that the herb is an antispasmodic and may indicate nervous tension, which can most certainly relate to these conditions. If IV The Emperor is chosen, one's digestion and eating habits may be affecting the skin or sleep, since the herb atractylodes, depicted on the card, relates to digestion and assimilation,

3. The querent should shuffle the cards face down while considering three to five possibilities that will offer ways of contemplating or healing the condition symbolized by the primary subject card or cards. Three to five cards should be drawn and placed face down under the subject card(s).

4. The first card on the left of the querent is turned over and the querent is again requested to describe what she or he sees and to associate freely the image on the card in light of a possible way to relate to or resolve the condition in question. The guide can assist as needed, drawing on knowledge about the card or the herb and its relevance to the querent's subject.

The querent is encouraged to explore any aspect of his or her thoughts and feelings. The guide may occasionally participate by adding thoughts on the card's relevance, but primarily the purpose of the guide is to encourage the querent to go deeper into his or her thoughts and feelings. The guide's questions can help in exploring some aspect of the card's significance in relation to the problem.

The herbal ally can be directly related to the querent's condition, though more often it represents a general therapeutic category from which other herbs and therapies may be chosen. For instance, if the herbal ally were the warming and stimulating herb cayenne pepper, as depicted on VIII Strength, more exercise and mental or physical stimulation may be suggested. It could also suggest the use of warming stimulants as an aid to treating a physical or emotional imbalance. If the individual is in a weakened and fatigued state, cayenne may in itself be too harsh and stimulating, but the aspect of warmth and improved circulation would certainly be helpful.

In this way, each card is turned over in succession and examined one by one, implying to the querent that there are a number of ways that he or she can treat the condition. The guide may offer suggestions and exercises based on what the cards and the querent disclose.

5. If there are further questions, such as what might be the cause or outcome of the condition, further cards can be selected and interpreted.

6. In conclusion, the guide may help the querent formulate an appropriate affirmation, meditation, psychological exercise, or dietary or herbal regime. The herbs may be drawn from all the cards selected during the session. One may not necessarily use the ally herbs, as they may not be appropriate to physiological needs. Rather, herbs based on the therapeutic approach suggested by the cards may be used.

Part of the closing may include presenting the querent with a tape recording of the session, an affirmation, a meditation or spiritual exercise card, an herbal talisman. The querent might be able to use an herbal essence, which can be taken while repeating silently the affirmation.

A complete set of the seventy-eight herbs of the Herbal Tarot and/or individual herbs may be purchased from Candis Cantin (see Where to Buy Herbs and Herbal Products at the end of the book).

Above all else, a session should be done in a spirit of play!

Medicine Wheel Spreads

by Lesley Tierra

The Medicine Wheel is a mirror, a reflection of all aspects of ourselves and of all of life. As a circle with no beginning and no end, it represents the Great Spirit, God, the Cosmos, encompassing all of life, known and unknown. It is delineated by four directions on the circumference, and the center point, or the source.

Each of the four directions represents a different aspect of ourselves. The south encompasses what is right before our eyes, the immediate present, and our emotional feeling nature. The west represents our inner world, dreams, intuition, and inner strength. The north includes our mental self, knowledge, wisdom, purification, and renewal. The east symbolizes seeing the whole, the overviews, and includes vision, foresight, and farsightedness.

Each direction is represented by an animal, the attributes of which help give a picture or understanding of that direction. In the south is the mouse, the west has the bear, the north the buffalo, and the east the eagle. The center of the wheel is the source, Godhead, the point from which all else emerges. It also represents our higher selves, our individual connection with God.

A wheel is always turning, and thus we are able to move from point to point on it. The different aspects flow into and out of each other as in a dance. If we stop the wheel at a point in time, we can use the qualities of the four directions to gain information about ourselves and our lives.

The Medicine Wheel Spreads can be used as mirrors of the major aspects of ourselves, emotional, mental, spiritual, inner, physical, and visionary. They can encompass the present, past and future, our conscious, subconscious and superconscious and our material, intuitive, wisdom selves and spiritual selves.

Major Arcana cards can indicate herbal allies, while suits have elemental, physiological, and herbal associations:

Major Arcana: Totem or symbolic herb; the connection with your Higher Self
Pentacles: Earth element; nourishment, digestion, assimilation, elimination
Cups: Water element; urinary system, reproductive organs, sexuality; urinary tonics, diuretics, aphrodisiacs
Wands: Fire element; energy, blood, circulation; stimulants, carminatives, hemostatics
Swords: Air element; nervous and respiratory systems; nervines, antispasmodics, expectorants

For all the Medicine Wheel spreads, shuffle the cards until you feel they are in perfect order. While shuffling, request to be shown more clearly your inner nature and to be guided to the areas that need more attention and work. When the cards feel "set," place the top card in the center, the next card under the center card, the third to the left, the fourth above, and the fifth to the right. The four outer cards now define a circle around the middle card, and represent south, west, north, and east, respectively.

Medicine Wheel Moon Spread

The Medicine Wheel Moon Spread can be used to reflect on what is taking place at this moment in time inside yourself, or to help you see areas to work on to balance your personal wheel. It reflects your inner process, clarifying it and showing what areas of yourself need more attention and work to bring your being into dynamic wholeness. Often when we clarify what is truly going on inside of us in all areas, our questions are immediately answered and our future direction is indicated.

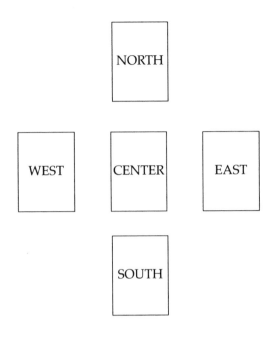

Medicine Wheel Spread

This spread incorporates all aspects of the wheel, using the directions to represent your emotional, intuitive, intellectual, and visionary natures. These all flow together, as all aspects of our nature are interconnected and interdependent.

The **Center card** represents you in an integrated way in the present moment. It is a consolidated overview of all the directional qualities and traits. It represents your awareness of connecting to the Higher Self. This card may be read first as an introduction and mood-setter, or after the reading as a synthesis of the entire reading, or both. It is the main symbolic card of where you are in your life. It doesn't mean that this is who you are in totality; rather, it represents the overall aspect of the self and the major issues that are in play or are being worked out at this time in your life. It can suggest how to do this work, hint at what more needs to be focused on, or give direction for where you are headed.

The **South card** represents your emotional nature and describes the qualities or directions of your present feelings, both known and hidden.

A Major Arcana card here represents strong feelings about the area that the card represents. These feelings are intense and influential, whether or not you are consciously aware of them.

A sword signifies an intellectual approach to your feelings: perhaps you think about them more than feel them, or you need to give them a lot of thought. Your feelings may need to be tempered with your inner wisdom and reason. A sword could represent searching for the truth of your feelings, cutting away the old and useless while keeping that which is of value.

Wands give action to your feelings. You may be actively struggling with them, working through issues.

Since the cups represent our emotional nature, a cup here indicates unimpeded self-expression. A strong emotional nature or a specific emotional issue is being dealt with or needs to be faced. Getting in touch with your deep feelings is appropriate. Cups here also represent feelings about your relationships with others.

Pentacles in the south signify a grounded or physical expression with respect to the emotions. Perhaps the emotions relate to worldly affairs or would be more satisfying if focused in that direction.

A reversed card indicates the emotion is unknown to you or others, hidden or suppressed. It could mean that working inside yourself on your feelings is more appropriate than displaying them to the world.

The **West card** symbolizes your inner world, revealing what is really going on inside you, known and unknown. It includes your dreams, deep desires, hidden issues, and intuition. It incorporates your "shadow," as put forth by Jung, the dark side that needs to be acknowledged. This card can also represent your inner strengths and your degree of introspection and inner work.

A Major Arcana card here indicates that an intense amount of energy is occurring on whatever inner levels the card represents. More introspection and inner work are taking place. The card specifies the attributes of your inner world and what direction your inner work is taking or should take, and it reflects your inner dreams and deep desires.

A sword in the west denotes that you are mentally processing what is occurring within or that you need to take a more mental approach to your inner situation, separating what is real from what is unreal. Perhaps talking about it would be helpful.

A wand indicates that you are actively working inside yourself, experiencing your dreams, acting on your intuition. On the other hand, you may need to delve within yourself more actively or act on whatever your inward experience or intuition tells you.

A cup represents an emotional inner world or strong feelings about your dreams or hidden nature. It may indicate that you could express your emotions about your dreams and intuitions more fully. A cup could also symbolize your relationship to your innermost self and your inner relationship to others.

Pentacles indicate concrete, physical, or material experience and expression. Perhaps it is time to bring your dreams and inner awareness to worldly affairs. A pentacle could mean that you are working out your worldly affairs through introspection.

A reversed card states that your inner world is known more to you than to others or may indicate that your issues run so deep that your inner life is hidden even from you. It can also state that your inner work is to remain inside of you rather than taking expression in your outer life.

The **North card** represents your mental life. It includes your mental concepts, ideas, reasons, intellectual pursuits, values, and wisdom nature. Since matter and experiences are form given to thought, they show us how we think and mentally approach and even create our lives.

A Major Arcana card here symbolizes intense mental processing, abilities, concepts, ideas, or work occurring in the area that card represents. It could indicate that more energy needs to be given to thinking something through or tapping into your wisdom nature.

A sword card in the north strengthens mental clarity and its intensity. Thinking, intellectualizing, discriminating, or using your inner wisdom is indicated. Perhaps you are very verbal or are involved in communication or you express your thoughts and ideas freely.

A wand in the north denotes that action is, or needs to be, given to your thoughts and ideas. Acting on your wisdom, ideas, philosophical beliefs, or mental concepts is appropriate.

Cups indicate you may feel your inner wisdom more than you think about it. Perhaps your intellectual approach is too emotional or, on the other hand, perhaps it needs to be softened or balanced with your feelings. You may relate to others more intellectually.

A pentacle card in the north indicates a concrete physical

approach to your intellectual concepts and wisdom. Your concepts and ideas can be put into form or physically manifested.

A reversed card signifies that your mental and intellectual process occurs inwardly, hidden to others and possibly unknown to you. It may also indicate that an internalized process needs to occur with your thoughts or that more inward focus on your wisdom or philosophy is necessary before outward work is done with them.

The **East card** represents your visionary nature, that part of you that sees where you are going and envisions a more perfect or balanced state of being. Its qualities of clarity and farsightedness know the overall picture, your inner self, life, and your relationship to the outer world and the cosmos.

A Major Arcana card here intensifies these qualities in whatever ways the card represents. Work is occurring or will occur in those areas of your visionary self.

A sword in the east suggests an intellectual or philosophical approach to your visions and overview. Communicating your insights or bringing your personal wisdom more into play within the realm of your visions may be appropriate or discrimination may be necessary in terms of your visions and overall view.

A wand denotes action taken on your insights, plans, or overall vision.

Cups denote that you approach your vision emotionally, that your overall awareness is more a feeling nature, that incorporating your emotions into your overall picture is appropriate or that your emotions are concerned with relationships to others.

Pentacles state that it is time to put into physical form or expression your insights and visions.

A reversed card suggests work on your insight, foresight, and vision. Your overall view and awareness may still be cloudy to you, working itself out deep within and not yet ready to be known or put forth, even to yourself.

The Inner Teachers Moon Spread

Center card: Your physical-spiritual balance and overview teacher of all other aspects of your being.

South card: The child-teacher within; what to nurture, express, and trust within yourself and life.

West card: Your deepest desires; your intuitive teacher.

North card: The wisdom teacher within; your philosophical beliefs and concepts.

East card: Your spiritual teacher; your strengths, clarity, and path.

The Consciousness Moon Spread

Center card: An overall picture of you presently; you as an integrated being.

South card: The qualities of the conscious self or the present focus.

West card: The subconscious self or the introspective process.

North card: The superconscious self or inner wisdom.

East card: The result, outcome, vision, or overview.

The Time Line Moon Spread

This layout is an overview statement of your life: past, present, and future.

Center card: The whole self and how you manifest yourself with the energies of each of the directions—your present awareness, your past, your inner guidance, and the options for the future.

South card: The present and how you are at the moment— your present awareness and focus.

West card: The past; an inner summation of all that has gone before you.

North card: The wisdom, guidance or advice that is coming to you; what you need to do in order to manifest your vision for the future.

East card: The future card and the overview as to what is possible in the future and what can result from the present elements involved.

The Overview Moon Spread

Center card: Your totem herb, the symbolic message of who you are as a summation of all your parts in the current moment.

South card: Your physical and material world, the present and your emotional nature.

West card: Your inner world, the past and your intuition.

North card: Your mental world, the path in this life, including a summation from past and present and view of moving into the future.

East card: The outer world, vision, the future and your spiritual nature.

Medicine Wheel Sun Spread

The Medicine Wheel Sun Spread applies the direction qualities of the medicine wheel to answering a specific question or giving insight on a specific issue. When shuffling the cards for this spread, focus intensely on the question being asked or the issue to be clarified.

Center card: Where you are now; an overview of the question and how it affects you in all ways.

South card: Feelings you should explore; feelings that you hold about the issue or problem.

West card: Your inner focus; dreams and intuition as they interact with the question.

North card: Wisdom and intellectual understanding of the situation; the mental attitude that may be beneficial.

East card: The overall answer to the question. An upright card could mean yes or could indicate what can enlighten the situation or change it, while a reversed card can mean no or that it is not yet time for a clear answer.

A reversed card in any other position suggests that the issue is being worked out inwardly or should be worked on within or by yourself. It is not time for outward action, expression, or manifestation.

Sacred Herb Spread

by Lonnie Packard

The growth of plants shows us how our own growth progresses. From the roots come our foundations, the love and nurturing of the great Earth Mother. From the stem our vitality and energy are expressed, and from the branches that spread out come our ability to expand and reach out to the world around us through our emotions, talents, and communication. From the branches the leaves emerge and awaken our ability to take in the light from Father Sun, which arouses within us our courage. The flowers are our ability to express love, and the fruit is where we find our joy and rapture.

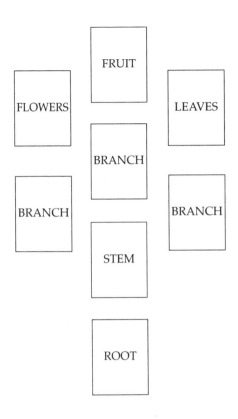

Sacred Herb Spread

Root: My foundation.
Stem: How I express my vitality and energy.
Branches: My emotional expression, my source of talents and creativity, my ability to communicate.
Leaves: My courage.
Flowers: How I express love.
Fruit: Where I find joy.

Glossary

Alterative: Tends to restore normal health; cleanses and purifies the blood.

Analgesic: Relieves pain when taken orally.

Antibacterial: Destroying or stopping the growth of bacteria.

Antibiotic: Inhibits growth of or destroys microorganisms.

Antipyretic: Dispels heat, fire, and fever.

Antispasmodic: Relieves spasms of voluntary and involuntary muscles.

Aroma therapy: Use of the fragrance of herbs to induce states of being for body/mind/spirit. For further information on aromatherapy read *The Art of Aromatherapy*, by Robert B. Tisserand.

Aromatic herbs: Herbs that contain volatile, essential oils which have various therapeutic values. Many aromatic herbs are used in incense or "smudging," including sage, juniper, and lavender. Others are used in flavorings such as oils of lemon or orange. Some, such as peppermint, are used for indigestion. Eucalyptus, for example, is used as an inhalant. Other uses are in ointments, cosmetics, and perfumes.

Astringent: Firms tissues and organs; reduces discharges and secretions.

Aura: An invisible, radiant light that surrounds the physical body. Auras exist around all life forms and have different colors, sizes, and densities depending on the state of being of each individual. Some people have developed the ability to see auras.

Bitter tonics: Bitter herbs that in small amounts stimulate digestion and otherwise help regulate fire in the body. They clear toxins as well.

Calmative: Herbs that have a soothing and sedating action.

Chakra: Spiritual energy centers that are outside of the body but connected to different parts of the body. The first chakra is connected at the tailbone area; the second just below the navel; the third at the area of the solar plexus; the fourth at the heart area; the fifth at the throat area; the sixth at the forehead or third eye area; the seventh at the top of the head. *See also* Kundalini.

Cholagogue: Promotes the flow of bile into the intestines.

Cystitis: Inflammation of the urinary bladder.

Decoction: This is a very potent way of preparing herbal medicine from the roots and/or bark of plants. It is much stronger than a beverage tea. Place one ounce of cut up dried root and/or bark in two cups of water. With the lid on the pot allow the herbs to gently boil for ten to twenty minutes. Another way of decocting herbs is to place the ounce of herbs in a pint jar, cover it and let it sit at room temperature for seven or eight hours. Strain out the herb(s) and discard solids, keeping the fluid.

Demulcent: Soothes, protects, and nurtures internal membranes.

Devas: Spiritual beings who are the guardians and protectors of the natural world; plant beings and spirits.

Diaphoretic: Causes perspiration and increases elimination through the skin.

Digestant: Contains substances that aid in digestion.

Diuretic: Promotes activity of kidney and bladder; increases urination.

Emetic: Induces vomiting.

Emmenagogue: Herbs that promote menstruation, usually causing it to occur and sometimes increasing the flow. These have been used to induce abortions, but extreme caution is advised. All emmenagogues, when taken in sufficient quantities to cause abortion, have other strong effects on the body. No emmenagogues should be taken when a woman wants to be pregnant. They are commonly used to help regulate the menstrual cycle. Some herbs with strong emmenagogue properties include juniper berries, black cohosh, angelica, and wild ginger.

Expectorant: Promotes discharge of phlegm and mucus from lungs and throat.

Eyewash: An herbal infusion, strained very carefully and thoroughly. Dose is two or three drops in each eye.

Hemostatic: Stops the flow of blood; type of astringent that stops internal bleeding or hemorrhaging.

Herbal essence: Put one drop of an herbal tincture in one ounce of pure water. It is best to store an herbal essence in a dark dropper bottle. Shake the bottle before using and then place four drops under the tongue. Hold it there for sixty seconds. An appropriate affirmation may be said or meditation may be commenced.

Homeopathic potency: The measure of strength of a homeopathic remedy. A tincture, called the mother tincture, is diluted, one part to 100 parts neutral solution. The result is percussed, or shaken, and is called "first potency." The first potency is diluted one part to 100 parts neutral solution and percussed to obtain the second potency, and so on.

Homeopathy: A system of medicine developed in the eighteenth and nineteenth centuries by Samuel Hahnemann, based on dilution of extracts of substances. The diluted solutions are taken according to the law of similars; symptoms caused by a undiluted essence are treated in minute doses. For example, undiluted onions cause crying; a diluted solution of onion is good for watery eyes and runny nose. *See also* Homeopathic potency.

Infusion: An infusion is a medicinally potent way of preparing herbs and is much stronger than the beverage tea that most people take. With leaves and flowers: place an ounce of the leaves and/or flowers in a quart jar and cover with a quart of boiling water. Allow the herbs to steep for twenty minutes to two hours depending on the herbs and the strength desired. Strain out the herbs and take up to three cups of liquid per day. Store the unused portion in the refrigerator. With seeds, place one ounce of dried seed and berries in a pint jar. Fill the jar to the top with boiling water, cover it, and allow it to infuse for thirty minutes. Rosehips and hawthorn berries may be infused for up to three hours.

Kundalini: The spiritual energy lying dormant in the base of the spine. When awakened in a conscious way, one's spiritual expansion flows through the various chakra points.

Laxative: Promotes bowel movement.

Nervine: Strengthens the functional activity of the nervous system; may be stimulant or sedative.

Nutritive: Increases weight and density, nourishes the body.

Plaster: Like a poultice, but the herbal materials either are placed between two thin pieces of linen or are combined in a thick base material and then applied to the skin.

Poultice: A warm, moist mass of powdered or macerated herbs that is applied directly to the skin to relieve inflammation, blood poisoning, venomous bites and eruptions, and to promote proper cleansing and healing of the affected area.

Sedative: Herbs that calm or tranquilize by lowering functional activity of an organ or body part.

Smudging: Dried, crushed, aromatic herbs such as sage, mugwort, sweet grass, and others are placed in a fire-safe receptacle such as a clay pot or seashell and then ignited. The smoke is wafted on to the self, those present, objects, or the space which is to be blessed, purified, and protected.

Stimulant: Increases internal heat, dispels internal chills, and strengthens metabolism and circulation.

Talisman: A pouch containing herbs or other special objects that help the wearer to manifest the spiritual principles s/he wishes to embrace.

Tea: A standard water-based herbal preparation. Use one teaspoon of dried herb per cup of boiling water. Let it steep from five to twenty minutes, depending on the strength desired. Some of the volatile herbs that extract easily in water are chamomile, shepherd's purse, lemon balm, lobelia, ginger, fennel seeds, and dill seeds. For stronger medicinal teas, see *Decoction* and *Infusion* .

Tincture: Herbs prepared and extracted in brandy, vodka, other liquors, or apple cider vinegar. Use fresh plants whenever possible. Fill a jar with one to four ounces of the chopped herb(s) and then pour in liquor or vinegar until the herbs are completely immersed. The liquid should be about an inch above the herbs. Label the jar with the date, the name of the plant, and the type of liquid used. Place the jar in a dark cabinet and shake it daily. Allow it to extract for two to six weeks or more. It is best to put up tincture on the new moon and strain it off on the full moon so that the drawing power of the waxing moon will help extract the herbal properties.

Tonic: Stimulates nutrition and increases the tone of the system. Tonics are usually given during absence of illness. Some tonic herbs are ginseng, dong quai, slippery elm, astragalus.

Vulnerary: Assists in healing wounds by protecting against infection and stimulating cell growth.

BIBLIOGRAPHY

Arroyo, Stephen. *Astrology, Psychology, and the Four Elements.* Reno: CRCS Publications.

Ballentine, Rudolph. *Diet and Nutrition: A Wholistic Approach.* Himalayan Press.

Beyerl, Paul. *The Master Book of Herbalism.* Canaan, NH: Phoenix Publishing Co.

Case, Paul Foster. *The Tarot.* Richmond, VA: Macoy Publishing Co.

Connelly, Dianne. *Traditional Acupuncture: The Law of the Five Elements.* Columbia, MD: Center of Traditional Acupuncture.

Crowley, Aleister. *Tarot Divination.* York Beach, ME: Samuel Weiser.

Culpepper, Nicholas. *Culpepper's Complete Herbal.* Philadelphia: W. Foulsham and Co.

Frawley, David. *Ayurvedic Healing.* Sandy, UT: Passage Press.

Frawley, David, and Ladd, Dr. V. *The Yoga of Herbs.* Detroit: Lotus Press.

Greer, Mary K. *Tarot For Yourself.* North Hollywood, CA: Newcastle Publishing Co.

Grieve, Mrs. M. *A Modern Herbal.* St. Edmundsbury Press.

Griggs, Barbara. *Green Pharmacy: A History of Herbal Medicine.* New York: Viking Press.

Gurudas. *The Spiritual Properties of Herbs.* San Rafael, CA: Cassandra Press.

Hall, Manly P., *The Tarot.* Los Angeles: Philosophical Research Society.

Hoffman, David. *The Holistic Herbal.* Findhorn Press.

Hogart, Ron. *Lecture Series on Astrology.* Los Angeles: Philosophical Research Society.

Holmes, Peter. *The Energetics of Western Herbs.* Boulder: Artemis.

Kaplan, Stuart. *The Encyclopedia of Tarot.* Vols. I, II, III. Stamford, CT: U.S. Games Systems.

Lotterhand, Jason. *The Thursday Night Tarot.* North Hollywood, CA: New Castle Publishing Co.

Mayberry, Richard. *The New Age Herbalist.* New York: Macmillan Publishing Co.

Nichols, Sallie. *Jung and Tarot.* York Beach, ME: Samuel Weiser.

Reid, Daniel P. *Chinese Herbal Medicine.* Boston: Shambhala.

Rose, Jeanne. *Herbs and Things.* New York: Grosset and Dunlap.

Rudhyar, Dane. *The Astrology of Personality.* New York: Doubleday and Co.

Teeguarden, Ron. *Chinese Tonic Herbs.* Japan Publications, Inc.

Tierra, Lesley. *Herbs of Life.* Trumansburg, NY: Crossing Press.

Tierra, Michael. *Planetary Herbology. Detroit:* Lotus Press.

Tierra, Michael. *The Natural Remedy Bible.* New York: Pocket Books; Simon and Schuster.

Tierra, Michael. *The Way of Herbs.* New York: Pocket Books; Simon and Schuster.

Turner, Kristina. *The Self Healing Cookbook.* Grass Valley, CA: Earth Tones Press.

Wanless, James. *New Age Tarot.* Carmel, CA: Merrill-West Publishing.

Willmott, Jonathan Clogstoun. *Western Astrology and Chinese Medicine.* New York: Destiny Books.

Special thanks to the Temple of Living Prayer in Sacramento for their contributions to the spiritual perspectives on plants and the affirmations.

Study Herbs at Home with Michael Tierra

The East West Herbal Distance Learning Course is a comprehensive thirty-six lesson course integrating Western, Chinese and Ayurvedic herbalism. It is focused around the traditional systems of diagnosis by interrogation, observation, listening and palpation. Upon completion, the student is given a graduation certificate from the East West Herb School.

Please visit our website or contact us for more information: www.planetherbs.com

East West Herbal Correspondence Course
P.O. Box 275
Ben Lomond, CA 95005
800-717-5010
herbcourse@planetherbs.com

Herbal Tarot Home Study Course

Learn the skills of tarot, herbs and astrology. The lessons are geared for the beginner as well as those who have some knowledge of these subjects and want to work at integrating the symbolic/energetic meaning of the Herbal Tarot so that it can be used as an effective tool for bringing into harmony body/mind/spirit. The course includes different spreads, rituals, meditations, herbal formulas, recipes, and a wholistic view of healing using the four elements of earth, water, fire and air. Write for free information:

Candis Cantin-Packard
Herbal Tarot Course
P.O. Box 1445
Placerville, CA 95667

Where to buy Herbs and Herbal Products

Herbal Tarot Essences, Extracts, and Talismans

Candis Cantin-Packard
P.O. Box 1445
Placerville, CA 95667
Write for a free brochure

Michael Tierra's Herb Formulas

www.planetherbs.com
www.vitacost.com

Chinese Herbs

Great China Art Co.
857 Washington Street
San Francisco, CA 94108
(415) 982-2195
Fax: (415) 982-5138

May Way Trading Company
1338 Mandela Parkway
Oakland, CA 94607
800-909-2828
www.mayway.com

Bulk Herbs

www.mountainroseherbs.com

Index

218